THE RECONSTITUTION OF IRELAND

Seamus McKenna

Also by Seamus McKenna

Non fiction

The Omicron Forex Trading Manual (2012)

Chickens, Hurling, and a famous bootmaker: Broadcast by the author on Sunday Miscellany (New Writing for Radio), RTE Radio 1, on 21st July 2024.

Fiction

The Maker's Name, a novel (2024)

THE RECONSTITUTION OF IRELAND

A nation's progress, told through the letters pages of The Irish Times

Seamus McKenna

The lucid and compelling prose that impressed a succession of Irish Times Letters Editors over 47 years.

Audacity Publications
Maynooth

Audacity Publications

32A Silken Vale,
Maynooth,
Co. Kildare
Ireland.

Copyright © Seamus McKenna

Seamus McKenna has asserted his right under the
Copyright and Related Rights Act 2000 to be identified as
the author of this work.

British Library Cataloguing in Publication Data:
A catalogue record for this book is available from the
British Library.

ISBN: 978-1-7385410-4-1

**Printed and bound in the UK
by IngramSpark**
Milton Keynes,
UK

Dedicated to Marilyn, Shane, and Kate.

Contents

Introduction 1
   An eclectic range of subjects 2
   There's room for whimsey too 3

Divorce 5
   Divorce in a country that does not allow it 7
   A terrible disturbance 10

Psychological conditioning 14
   A sad place 15
   Sexual abuse 16

Morality and law 19
   Glorification of violence 24
   The Airport 25
   'Aggressive secularism' 28
   Religious symbols in public places 36
   The teaching of science 37
   John McGahern and religion 38
   The Catholic right wing 40
   Oaths of office, and other swearing 44

What's the alternative? 47
   Blasphemy law 50

Religious control of education in Ireland 53
Origins and comparisons 53
The church goes legal 58
The state's responsibility to education 61
Forum on school patronage 63
The "integrated curriculum" 67
Divestment, or the lack of it 69
Discrimination in education 72
The archaic patronage system in Irish education 75
A sectarian school system? 78
The baptism barrier 82
Comparative religion studies 86
Advances undermined 91

Institutional child abuse 93
A celibate clergy 94
Government reports on abuse in state institutions 99
Taoiseach Enda Kenny excoriates the Catholic Church 104

Abortion in Ireland 113
Frozen embryos 114
The campaign to repeal the Eight Amendment 123

Sinn Féin 128
The murder of Terence McKeever 128
Election success 131
Gerry Adams and the N-word 133

Heineken cup 2011, Temple Street Children's hospital 136

Orla Tinsley 139

Cystic Fibrosis; the terrible condition 143
Hare coursing 145
Joke of the week 147
The financial crisis of 2008 150
    An unpleasant precedent 150
    Bust and austerity 153
    Recovery 155
Science in the island of saints and scholars 158
General election 2011 161
Gun violence in the USA 163
Why the Celtic Tiger took so long to arrive 166
Would Fianna Fáil survive? 168
Clamping at the tram terminus carpark 171
Ireland's approach to public service transportation 173
Psychology and belief 175
United States politics 178
    The accession of Barack Obama 178
    Leo Varadkar in the USA for St. Patrick's Day 180
    Donald Trump 182
    Trump's visit to Ireland 184
Seasonal lamb 189
Call for peace in Ukraine 192
Ursula von der Leyen and war in the Middle East 195
    War in Gaza 195
    Germany and Judaism in recent history 196

- Evil in uniform 197
- Real horror 200
- Other victims 202

Ireland in the European Union 206
- The Maastricht Treaty 207
- Migration 209
- French President Macron and European renewal 212
- Neutrality and The European Union 214

The physics of raindrops 215

AIB bank and remuneration 224
- Directors' pay 224
- Bonus payments 226

Brussels, and airline practices 228

Energetic, resourceful, and hard-working students 231
- Mary Hanafin, Minister for Education 2004 and 2008 234

Noise pollution 236

China 242
- Visit of Xi Jinping to Ireland, 2012 245

The Waterford Blaa 249

Wine bottles 253

Censorship of books and other publications 256

And on the subject of books… 259

About the author 261

Introduction

Instructions to those who write a letter to the editor of The Irish Times are precise: avoid preamble; keep them short; write on one subject; and supply your name and address, which they will append to your effort if it does appear in the paper; they will not print letters written over a pseudonym. They will contact you to confirm that you are the person who sent it in, but they will not discuss the contents or give any estimate about when or even if it might be published. Getting to that stage is difficult, but many people have achieved it. High profile individuals, whether in politics, business, the arts, or academia, will be given priority. It is well known that, after those submissions have been catered for, getting a share of the space that is left is difficult.

I do not have any kind of an inside track. Up to this point there has never been any contact between me and the letters editors or their staffs, apart from phone calls to me in the early days to confirm that I was the writer. Now they seem to recognise my email address. I do not know the thought processes of those who choose letters for publication, except to realise that, perhaps, it is a subjective and varying business.

With practice I have come to realise that there might be principles that could be followed to increase the chances of publication. For example, it seems to help if the email is composed and sent immediately one becomes aware of the trigger for it. This will often involve breaking off from one's breakfast reading to do it. Keep the letters shortish; between two hundred and three hundred words seems to be optimum.

I cannot remember what it was that motivated me to send in my first letters, but the archive shows that it was sometime in the nineteen-seventies. That's because the first one to be found there was published on 4th November 1978. That's 46 years ago at this writing. Did I compose them then in longhand? I can't remember, but they were certainly not sent in by email.

An eclectic range of subjects

Over the years I have contributed missives on a large range of subjects: the calculations involved in working out the speed of raindrops when they hit a surface; hare coursing; divorce, or the absence of it in the Ireland of the time; the European Economic Community (EEC), which was the forerunner of the EU; the European Union itself; bank directors' pay; business class flights on busy short haul routes; politics; economics; international affairs; noise pollution; science in education; general education.

In more recent times there were commentaries on abortion, including on the campaign to repeal the Eighth Amendment to the constitution, which at that time contained a ban on abortion; child abuse reports; the future of the Seanad (the Irish upper house of parliament); random mass shootings in the USA; residential property prices; the bailout after the economic crash of 2008; freedom of speech; Irish military neutrality; Brexit. But readers of this collection will quickly realise that there is a preponderate focus on one subject: the question of the separation of church and state in Ireland.

Within that category there are letters on the rights of minorities in a true democracy; the religiously driven constitutional ban on divorce (now gone); the Judeo-Christian attitude to violence, and its possible effects on children; clear calls for a secular state; religious attitudes to the freezing of embryos; defence of secularism from charges of it being "aggressive"; removal of the arrangement where churches have management of more than 90% of Irish state-funded schools; child abuse by religious and the protection of the perpetrators by the church; legislation on blasphemy; the damaging effects of enforced celibacy as a condition of becoming a priest, a monk, or a nun of the Catholic Church; religious discrimination in Irish schools; abortion and all it entailed in the years of letter writing, including the X case (where a girl of 14 who became pregnant after being raped was refused permission to travel to the UK to have a termination), freedom to travel for an abortion and, eventually, the Campaign to Repeal the Eighth; religion and sex education; and taking God out of the oath that's required for public office in Ireland.

There is still much work to be done in regard to separation of church and state. At the time of this writing, more than 90% of all Irish primary schools, which are funded by the state, are nevertheless under the management of religious institutions. This situation is wholly inappropriate in a modern, democratic republic.

More recently letters from me have appeared under the headings of "Appeasing Russian aggression will not bring peace", and on the subject of Donald Trump and his visits to Ireland.

There's room for whimsey too

I realised that, from time to time, the editors of the Irish Times liked their letter writers to be a little bit whimsical. That's where the discussion on the wine bottle cork and its alternative, the screw cap, came from, and the lauding of books for, among other things, providing a prop for the morning paper when one is having one's breakfast.

Of course, there were challenges sent in, and published, to the letters I wrote, and it would have been terribly disappointing if this had not been the case. There is nothing worse than being ignored, after all.

Between 2017 and 2023 I submitted 250 letters to the editor of the Irish Times. Some 60 of those were published. That's a publication success rate of 24%.

Did the published letters make a difference? I like to think they did, on some level. Constant dripping wears the stone and, particularly in the case of a true separation of church and state in Primary education, the status quo is so entrenched that it requires a constant searching for new ways to state the case for such separation. I am grateful to the Irish Times for providing me with a platform for the arguments that I made.

The letters in this collection are accompanied by essays on the topic concerned, including details of my personal situation at the time they were written.

Seamus McKenna
Maynooth, September 2024

Chapter ONE

Divorce

When I was twenty-one my father had a brain haemorrhage. He went into a coma, remained breathing for only a few days, and died without ever regaining consciousness. My poor mother had not been well since she had contracted tuberculosis some eighteen years previously, when she would have been about twenty-seven, and when I was three. On my father's death, in January 1971, she went into further decline. She outlived him for a mere three months.

I got married that same year. Matrimonial preparation in 1971 in Ireland for the majority of the population, as they had been born into the Catholic religion, consisted of visits to one or another parish priest. At one stage my Fiancée's PP asked me to leave the room so that he could talk to her alone. She told me afterwards he wanted to know if she was under any duress to get married. Was she pregnant? She was just short of twenty-one years of age at the time.

In his normal working day this man made no bones of the fact that he regarded it as his right, indeed his duty, to visit all the public libraries in his parish so that he could remove or interfere with any books he regarded as being unsuitable. He would blank out the word "bloody", for example, wherever he found it. Anything even remotely sexual would definitely get the chop. This work of destruction was carried out with impunity.

We were presented with a booklet that purported to give helpful advice to people on the threshold of married life. It had been produced in the UK, and had plenty of colourful pictures, with generic details about such things as getting a mortgage, dealing with utility companies, and opening a joint bank account. In the middle there was a number of pages that had been glued together. Curiosity killed the cat, I know, but I could not resist treating those with the steam from a boiling kettle and prising them apart. What I discovered was that they dealt with the subject of contraception.

In the Irish Republic of 1971 the Roman Catholic hierarchy and its zealous followers, both clerical and lay, who inhabited most positions of power in the Civil Service, in education, in health and in all other branches of administration in the country, ensured that the church had a stranglehold on the lives of citizens. Everything had to be done to Catholic specifications. This meant there was a constitutional ban on both contraception and divorce. *Bunreacht na hÉireann*, or the Constitution of Ireland, the document that defined what could and could not be in the law of a country that had in its official title the word "Republic", had provisions that bound all citizens to the precepts of one particular religion!

The hard-right conservative element in the country, following the dictates of the Catholic Church, did everything in its power to persuade citizens not to vote the ban on divorce out of the Constitution. Efforts were made to persuade women that divorce was so much against their interest that if they voted to get rid of the ban, it would be like "turkeys voting for Christmas." This took no account of the poor unfortunate wives who were daily subjected to violence and coercive behaviour and who, because of this legal provision, were doomed to remain in that situation for the rest of their lives.

In the middle years of the last century the concept of coercive control was unknown. Happily, that situation has now been rectified.

Our marriage didn't last. We were both immature. We'd been married too young, and we paid the price. We must have surmounted the contraception prohibition by some means or other, because we had no children. The only option open to us was to separate, which we did. Then I met someone else. That someone else was Marilyn, who is now my wife of some 40 years. We have a son and a daughter who've been a boon to us for the whole of their lives, and who have now presented us with truly delightful grandchildren.

Divorce in a country that does not allow it

There were many reasons, at that stage of my life, and that of my new partner, why a divorce was necessary. We pondered the matter for a time. Then I read a book by a young solicitor, one Alan Shatter, called "Family Law in the Republic of Ireland", which he had published in 1977. Is that the same Alan Shatter, I hear you ask, who was later a Fine Gael Minister for both Justice and Defence at different times?

THE IRISH TIMES
24-28 TARA STREET, DUBLIN 2
FRIDAY, JUNE 13, 1986

DIVORCE
* * *

Sir, — I find what Voltaire said attractive: "I do not agree with what you say, but I will defend to the death your right to say it."

Occasionally one reads or hears proposals that do something more than generate disagreement. Sometimes one is genuinely frightened, as I was when I read Mary McAleese's letter (June 5th). She said that certain people should carry a Government health warning by way of a prohibition on remarriage. This is spine-chilling stuff. Is Ms McAleese arrogant enough to believe that she or the people who share her point of view are qualified to decide which individuals should have a fundamental human right and which should not?

Another scary assertion made by various members of the anti-divorce lobby is that it is alright to ignore the rights of minorities because it is difficult to legislate for every contingency; or because their Church says that a certain course of action has to forced upon those who want nothing whatever to do with that Church; or because of their perception of what is in the common good (a much abused phrase); or because it is expensive for the Government; or whatever.

These people want to interfere with our private thoughts and actions. I still, however, stick by what Voltaire said. Even from a practical point of view, it is better to know what is being put forward, in case it should creep up unawares. — Yours, etc.,
SEAMUS McKENNA,
Findrum,
Convoy,
Co Donegal.

The answer is yes. His book made all the difference. Among many other things, Shatter explained the concept of domicile. This is a legal term for the place where one lives, and intends, at the relevant time, to continue to live. Even then a divorce obtained when one was domiciled in another jurisdiction would be recognised in the Irish Republic. I suppose the government didn't want to become the laughing stock of the civilised world by having it otherwise.

Then a second, fortunate thing occurred. A job came up in the IDA (Industrial Development Authority) Donegal office for a Technical Officer, whose function it would be to supervise the maintenance of industrial estates and advance factories, and to give technical advice to industrialists who intended to establish their businesses in Donegal. At the time I was working as site manager on the Town of Youghal, Co. Cork, water supply and sewerage renewal scheme, having obtained a qualification in Civil Engineering a few years previously. This job in Donegal would suit me down to the ground.

The offices of the IDA were then situated in Lifford, within a short walk of the bridge over the river that defines the border with Northern Ireland. I could go and live in Strabane, Co. Tyrone, which is right on the other side of this bridge but, crucially, within the Northern Ireland component of the United Kingdom, and easily commute to Lifford.

I remember, at the time, there was another reason why I might like to live in that part of the world. It is well known for its traditional music. I saw myself enjoying many sessions involving fiddles, and that did indeed come to pass.

I applied for the job, and I got it. Then I went to live in Northern Ireland. Not in Strabane, as it happened, but in a flat in Marlborough Street in Derry, overlooking The Bogside. I got a solicitor in Derry, and applied, with my wife, for a consensual divorce. It was not necessary for her to change her domicile in order to take part in that process.

If there is one thing that characteries any civil legal proceeding it's that it consumes a prodigious amount of time. I settled in for a wait, making regular visits to the solicitor's offices, and down south to where my wife was living, in order to work out the details. On a daily basis I commuted to my work in Donegal, like a great many other people who lived in Derry. Some of the country's most enjoyable pubs, such as the Castle Bar, Peadar O'Donnell's, The Bogside Inn, and others, are in Derry, and I got to know them well. I enrolled for a two-year part-time course to gain a Higher National Certificate (HNC) in Computer Studies at the North West Regional College at Strand Road, Derry.

That was in the early 1980s. The so-called 'Troubles' were in full swing. The Provisional IRA and other militant groups were operating in the North, and riots were taking place in areas such as The Bogside. My flat, at the top of a large house just off the upper reaches of the steep hill that is Creggan Road, provided me with a bird's eye view of many of those dramatic events.

In October of 1980 a group of republican prisoners in Long Kesh prison in Northern Ireland went on hunger strike in pursuit of concessions that would allow them to wear their own clothes, and have free association while incarcerated. They wanted, in effect, to be treated as prisoners of war instead of being categorised as criminals.

After some 50 days without food one of them, Sean McKenna, whose family roots were in Co. Monaghan, in the Republic, fell into a coma. This got a lot of publicity. So much so that I was asked by British soldiers, flippantly, if I was related to him when I was stopped at border checkpoints between Donegal and Derry. Sean McKenna survived because there were concessions granted which allowed the Provisional IRA leadership to call off the hunger strike and then have him resuscitated.

The shooting of policemen and soldiers continued, however. Car and other bombs exploded. Over time I, like so many other people, began to see all this as a kind of background noise. I was not involved. Then a second hunger strike commenced, in early 1981, because the provisional IRA believed the concessions granted at the end of the first one were not being implemented. Tensions rose when Bobby Sands fell into a coma, but life continued as before.

A terrible disturbance

On the 5th of May 1981 I was wakened in the early hours. A terrible disturbance was underway. It had in the background a series of small bangs, the cumulative effect of which was to create a very loud and upsetting noise. I wanted to look out, to see what was happening, but was afraid to go near the window, even with the light off. As I was on the top floor of a three-storey house, then, the only way I could get a view was to stand on the bed at the side of the room away from the window, and look down, which I did. I saw that the awful noise was the result of lots and lots of individuals beating the roads and pavements with steel dustbin lids.

There was a lot of shouting. "Everybody out", was repeated over and over.

News of the death of Bobby Sands had come through.

I had been aware of the expression "quaking with fear". In the depth of that night I experienced the phenomenon in person. I decided to leave Derry the next morning via the Buncrana Road, which goes through commercial and middle-class areas, rather than via my usual, shorter, route through the Brandywell, which is more working-class.

Cometh the morning, I'm afraid, cometh the brave man. In the bright light of day I found myself wondering what I was worried about. I set off on my usual road out of town. A short way beyond Craigavon bridge I saw my first sign of trouble. Mattresses were burning on each side of the road, although it was possible to get through. Some way further on a man in a balaclava, although not obviously armed, beckoned me to stop. I was not going to risk disobeying him. As I slowed down he changed his posture and waved me on, for some reason.

There always seems to be something incongruous in this type of situation: a little further on I saw a lollypop man outside a school, complete with white coat and carrying the tool of his trade. He didn't seem to have too many takers though for his service of shepherding children across the road.

Soon I was at the border, and relieved to be there. Once in the office I phoned a friend of mine and asked to use his spare room for a while.

My decision to stay out of Derry was a good one. We heard horrendous stories, from both acquaintances and in the media, about the serious rioting that took place as more and more hunger strikers died. A total of ten men had agonising deaths before the protest was called off. When I went back, many weeks later, there were still vast piles of burnt-out vehicles at a great many of the cross roads.

In due course the divorce was granted, and my partner and I were free to get married. As we had used the law in the UK to get it we decided to marry in that jurisdiction too, and we did so in Uxbridge, London, in 1985.

It can be imagined the side I was going to take when the government of Ireland announced, in 1986, that it was to hold a referendum on a proposal to end the constitutional ban on divorce. There was considerable opposition to this mainly, but not exclusively, from people who wanted to follow the teachings of the Catholic Church on the matter. My position was plain: the ban was a terrible negation of the human rights of people who wanted to dissolve their marriages, but who did not have the resources or the opportunities that I had enjoyed when I solved my problem in that regard; people who knew nothing about Alan Shatter's book, or who would not have been in a position to absorb it if they had known about it. People who did not have the financial wherewithal to do what I had done. Ireland therefore was a two-tier society, and that was wrong.

In the event, that referendum was defeated. The constitutional ban remained, but not before I had the opportunity to air my views on the matter in the letters page of the Irish Times. It was a big, and sometimes acrimonious, debate. It will be seen from one of the letters below that one of my opponents in this was Mary McAleese, who was later to make her mark on history by becoming the 8th president of Ireland, and the second woman to hold that office, after Mary Robinson.

But the movement to change the Constitution so that divorce could become a reality in Ireland, and drag it into modern times, continued apace.

A ban on divorce never had the same impact on the national consciousness as had the total ban on abortion. The only common thread running though both was the fact that they were subjects that were expounded upon by the Catholic Church. The same went for the removal of the taint of illegality that adhered to homosexuality in Ireland until 1993, when it was decriminalised. Speaking in the Dáil at the time of the passing of the law that achieved this, the man who was to later become leader of the Labour Party, Eamonn Gilmore, had this to say:

"The sexual activities of consenting adults in the privacy of their home are a matter for the people concerned and should not be the business of the Dáil, the Garda or anybody else, including the peeping Toms of the self-appointed moral police from whom we hear a great deal nowadays."

In 1995 a second referendum on divorce was held. The run up to this also contained many bitter and divisive arguments. There was a legal challenge, which was successful, to the use of government funds to promote the removal of the ban, so that particular advertising had to stop.

Two years prior to the second referendum, Mother Teresa, the nun who many in Ireland regarded as a living saint, visited the country and was given the freedom of the City of Dublin. She used the occasion to bitterly attack those who were campaigning for divorce to be allowed. Her standing was somewhat damaged later when she urged Diana, Princess of Wales, who she had befriended, to get a divorce from Charles, Prince of Wales, and later King of Great Britain and Northern Ireland.

On 24 November 1995 the result of the new referendum was known. A majority had voted to remove the ban on divorce. This became law on 17 June 1996, and subsequent legislation defined the conditions under which divorce in Ireland could be granted.

THE IRISH TIMES

13 D'OLIER STREET, DUBLIN 2
FRIDAY, JUNE 20, 1986

* * *

DIVORCE

Sir, — One reason put forward for maintaining a ban on remarriage for people whose first marriage has failed is that it will withhold the opportunity from violent people of indulging in the battering of their spouses. I was exposed to this view twice in rapid succession last Sunday when I heard it first on the radio enunciated by Mr William Binchey, and then read it as part of a quote from the former Miss Ireland, Olivia Tracy, in a Sunday newspaper. She was explaining why she had come from a position of intending to vote yes to one in which she would probably abstain. She was described (described herself?) as "undecided".

I do not think that what follows is going to matter an awful lot vis a vis Mr Binchey, but I respect Ms Tracy's motives and I would appeal to her, and others, to think this line of reasoning through fully before they allow it to influence their decisions on polling day.

People who commit violent attacks on women and children will not be deterred one bit by a ban on remarriage.

I do not pretend to know what causes these attacks, but I believe that a person with psychopathic tendencies does not need to be in a formal relationship in order to batter his partner or a child of that partnership.

It is significant in this regard that in recent cases in the UK of child battering and neglect that led to death, the perpetrator was invariably described as a "boyfriend" and not a husband. I, myself, have known of cases where beatings have been handed out to girls during the courting stage. It amazed me that, in one case at least, the marriage went ahead anyway.

Of course, the great majority of marriage breakups occur in situations where violence is NOT a factor. I contend that the whole tragic question of battering is irrelevant to the present discussion. The people who have tendencies in this regard need professional help, and their partners need protection, whether they are in a formal married relationship, or not. — Yours, etc.,

SEAMUS McKENNA,
Findrum,
Convoy,
Co Donegal.

Chapter TWO

Psychological conditioning

Don't tell me it's easy to overcome conditioning. If a responsible adult has been telling you, from the time you became aware of what was around you, that there's a place in the sky where lives someone who always existed, who will always exist in the future, who can see everything, who knows your every thought, never mind your every action, and who takes a consuming interest in them, then that is what you will believe.

And why would you not take on board what these responsible adults tell you? After all, you depend on them to provide your food, to comfort you when that is needed, and to keep you safe.

Eventually you find that you're handed from the shelter of your loving mother into the care of others, in order that you can get an education. Then you begin to realise, if you lived in Ireland in the middle years of the last century, that a great many of these newly arrived responsible adults can turn out to be mocking, cynical, and violent. This cannot be right, you think, after a while. You might even start to question the ideas that they hand to you, like the one about the man in the sky who controls everything, or that when you were contributing for the 'Black babies' in Africa, that your pence were not necessary going to feed those poor devils, but rather to help to make them good Catholics whose souls could be saved by Baptism.

A sad place

The Ireland of the 1950s was a sad place. Apart from having an economy that didn't work, as evidenced by the massive emigration that took place then, it was ruled over by a dysfunctional conglomeration of a democratically elected, but religiously subservient, parliament, and an all-powerful cabal of bishops and cardinals of the Catholic Church, who made all the decisions of how the lives of the people should be regulated.

Corporal punishment in schools was legal in those years, and it was applied with vigour. In theory it was supposed to amount to nothing more than a few 'slaps' on the hand with a leather strap, but it extended in almost all schools to vicious assaults by grown adults on defenceless children. Eleven and twelve year old boys could be grabbed by the hair and have their heads beaten against the blackboard of the school room because they were unable to demonstrate knowledge of a mathematical theorem. Complaint to a parent of this kind of treatment would be useless. The authorities would not take any action if a father or mother had the temerity to visit the school, and most parents had themselves been brutalised in their day to the extent that they thought this kind of treatment was normal.

I read somewhere that Abraham Lincoln is on record as having said that his father and himself did not get on. I could relate to that. My father, it seems to me now, was frustrated by many things. He went to the pub every single night, where he drank large bottles of Guinness stout and glasses of whiskey, and played 45s. On Christmas Day, when all the pubs were officially closed, he would get the keys from the bar owner and he and his cronies would drink on that day too, using an honour system to pay the tab. When he came home he could be very aggressive, but a cousin of mine, whose family we only visited on Sunday afternoons when I was young, said to me a few years ago, when my father had been dead for many years:

"Your father was very harsh on ye," or words to that effect.

So it was not only the drink. He could, apparently, be sarcastic and antagonistic towards me even in front of them, when he was stone cold sober.

Sexual abuse

I was never sexually abused, and up to when I was quite mature I didn't even know there was such a thing. However, my memory, and my later knowledge, tells me that I came close to it on at least two occasions. The first time was when I was about five or six years old. Me and two other boys were waiting for the bus home from school when a youth came along on a bicycle.

"Why bother waiting for the bus and paying the fare?" he said. "I'll give you a lift home on my bike."

"But there are three of us," we said.

"It's okey. I'll be able to carry two of you half way home, I can come back for the other, and then do the same trick again to get you all home."

He took away the other two boys, and left me. Soon he was back.

"Before we go on the bike," he said, "why don't we take a walk in the De La Salle college grounds? They're just over there."

I agreed.

As we walked up the college avenue, he suggested that I put my hand in his pocket. I did that. It had a hole in the bottom that was big enough for that same hand to go through. I remember being surprised to find that I my fingers were on something that felt like the wrinkly bag that I knew was underneath my own willy.

A group of De La Salle brothers, in their black soutanes, came walking down the avenue.

"Quick, we have to hide," said the youth, which we did.

He must have got the wind up at that stage, because I remember nothing more. He probably brought me back to the bus stop, and I probably went home in the usual way. What is certain is that I was not traumatised in the slightest by any of this. I remember what I now recognise to be nothing more than a mild curiosity, that I should have been induced to put my hand into his pocket to feel what I did.

The second time was when I was between 16 and 17 years of age. I know this because The Naked Ape, by Desmond Morris, had just been published. The record shows that the year that happened was 1967.

I was still not 'getting on' with my father. I was also at the mercy of the kind of anxieties that beset many at that age. In any event, by some means or another, I was taken on for what would now be called counselling by a Catholic priest, who lived in a house in Waterford all by himself. Morris's book comes into the story because it was just out, I had read it, and my priest counsellor and I discussed it. We were both highly critical of the idea that there might be such a thing as evolution, which Morris takes for granted in his book. Of course God made everything, I believed then, and he made it in the form that it exists in the present.

There were other discussions of that sort, and our evenings would culminate in my kneeling in front of this man so that he could give me a blessing before I left for home. Boy, did that make me feel self-conscious.

We got around to talking about sex at an early stage. It was he who told me that women get very wet when they're sexually aroused. But the subject we kept coming back to, again and again, and then again, was my penis. Roughly now long was it when it was enlarged? Were there any veins to be seen on it? I answered these questions as best I could, until one evening it flashed across my mind that the next thing he'll want to do is have a look at it. Only a fleeting thought, that was, rapidly followed by the certainty that it was unthinkable that a highly respected man of the cloth would want to do such a thing. And he didn't.

But he did ask me, on one occasion, if I ever had the urge to have sex with animals!

I cannot remember how or when I decided to stop going to these sessions, but stop I did. In later years I had a discussion with another person who had also visited that priest in his house. My friend was fully convinced he was a paedophile.

None of those brushes with sexual abuse ever had any bearing on my religious belief. I was well and truly 'out' as a committed atheist long before there was even a hint that priests, lay teachers, scout masters, swimming coaches, even parents, had been obtaining sexual gratification at the shocking expense of children in their care.

For a time I would have said I was an agnostic, that I held open the possibility that there might have been a God, but I realise now this was only a step along the road to shaking off my early conditioning. Eventually I found it impossible to believe, and the only way to have conformed to the conventions practised by the majority of people around me would have been to perpetrate a fraud; to let on that I had faith.

Later still I read Richard Dawkins (The God Delusion), Christopher Hitchens (God is Not Great), Sam Harris (Letter to a Christian Nation), and Daniel Dennett (Darwin's Dangerous Idea). I found them to be a breath of fresh air, particularly Hitchens. There were others too, such as Luduvic Kennedy, who actually preceded the "Four Horsemen of the new Atheist movement", as they came to be known. Ludo wrote a book called All in the Mind: A Farewell to God. That was in 1999, some nine years before the publication of Dawkins's The God Delusion, which was the first Atheist book to gain a wide, global, readership.

When the Cloyne report, one of the first to throw light on the extent of the coverup by church authorities of the sexual abuse of children by priests, that has so comprehensively damaged religious belief in Ireland, was published, I could attack the idea that normal people in Ireland had some kind of responsibility for what those in authority had been doing. My belief was, and is, that the people in positions of authority in Ireland were so much in thrall to the church, and the ordinary people in the street has so little agency, that it made no sense to say that someone should have stood up to object to what was going on.

Chapter THREE

Morality and law.

The McGee case decision of the Supreme Court in 1973 was a landmark in Irish law. The interpretation, up to then, of a law of 1935 had made it impossible for Irish people to legally obtain contraceptives.

A 27-year-old mother of four, Mrs. Mary McGee, had taken a case in the High Court which sought a declaration that a part of the 1935 act, which banned the importation and sale of contraceptives, was invalid and contrary to the Constitution. Her case was special. She had suffered from toxaemia in each of her four pregnancies, and during the second she had had a cerebral thrombosis. Because of this her husband and herself had made up their minds not to have any more children. Mrs. McGee also thought that it would not be fair to either herself or her husband to discontinue having sexual intercourse, so they had decided on the use of contraception. This would be regarded as a most responsible attitude to adopt today, but was not so, at all, in the Ireland of 1973.

Mrs. McGee won her case on appeal to the Supreme Court. That could not have been the end of the matter, though, because legislation was then needed to implement the court's decision. There followed many convolutions in government and on the streets, including for a time a law that stipulated that contraception could only be provided to married couples, and then only on foot of a doctor's prescription! Earlier, in 1968, the then Pope, Paul VI, had issued a letter to his bishops, known as an encyclical, which instructed them that what he called artificial contraception, in other words anything that relied on mechanical or chemical inhibition of conception, such as condoms or the contraceptive pill, could not be used by Roman Catholics. The title of this directive was *"Humanae Vitae"*. Because it came from the Pope it was regarded as the very last word on the topic for the adherents of his religion.

Humanae Vitae did allow for methods of birth control that relied on only having intercourse during those times when the wife was infertile, which would be the case at a certain stage of the menstrual cycle. Great efforts were made by enthusiastic Catholics to develop methodologies that would be allowed under this heading, such as the rhythm method, the temperature method, the mucus inspection method, and methods that combine elements of all three. They are all difficult to implement with success, and for many people impossible.

Around the world, *Humanae Vitae* met with serious opposition, especially from those who were involved in work where overpopulation was an issue, or where HIV/AIDS had to be battled. Many of those who expressed their dissatisfaction with it were themselves pious and observant Catholics. The Church had its own way of dealing with them. In 1979, the Vatican declared that the well-known and widely-published Swiss theologian, Hans Kung, "has departed from the integral truth of Catholic faith, and therefore he can no longer be considered a Catholic theologian nor function as such in a teaching role." This effected his career as a university professor. The proximate cause was his questioning of the fallibility of the Pope, but his attitude to *Humanae Vitae* had also brought him to the attention of Rome, and not in a good way.

The thrust of my letter was to support the principle that, in a true democracy, minorities have rights. If the legislative ban on contraceptives was removed then Roman Catholics could follow the dictates of *Humanae Vitae*, and everyone else could trust to their own consciences in deciding what to do. Having to place religious principles in the law of the land reflects poorly on the ability of the church to maintain the faith of its adherents.

THE IRISH TIMES

13 D'OLIER STREET, DUBLIN 2
SATURDAY, NOVEMBER 4, 1978

MORALITY AND LAW

Sir, — While I agree with J. Brendan FitzGerald LL.B. when he suggests (October 28th) that the inherent logic of the Supreme Court decision in the McGee case could be questioned, I am very disappointed that he would not appear, from the general tone of his letter, to allow for the inherent logic of *Humanae Vitae* being similarly scrutinised. This type of reasoning always saddens me, and at times leads me to conclude that religious moralists just cannot be argued with, because they will not accept the rules of debate and have their basic premises subjected to the same treatment as those of their opponents.

Other matters contained in the letter disturb me, such as the writer advocating the framing of legislation around the social and religious traditions of a particular society. Mr FitzGerald says that "to do otherwise (than for legislators to choose a view which is in keeping with Catholic moral principles) is to choose a non-Catholic point of view and thereby discriminate against the majority".

I find this ludicrous. There would be no obligation on Catholics to avail themselves of facilities allowed under liberal laws. On the other hand, a restrictive code would very definitely discriminate against the so-called minority. It has always seemed to me to be a very poor sign of the authority of the Church when she has to rely on secular legislation to maintain the faith of her adherents.

Another question is the size of the minority. I find myself wondering about the integrity of people who blatantly and consistently violate the Church laws on contraception (and, yes, abortion) and still continue to allow themselves to be called Catholics. Are these people hypocrites, or are they, as I believe more likely, waiting for what they see as the almost certain relaxation of these dictates in the future? Only time will tell.—Yours, etc.,

SEAMUS McKENNA,
Ballinakina,
Halfway House,
Co Waterford.

That was in 1978. But the Papal encyclical in question has had nothing if not a long life. In October of 2014, some 36 years later, Dr. Damian O'Maonaigh argued that the precepts of *Humanae Vitae* had not been tried and found wanting. Instead, he said, it had been found difficult, and left untried. This, to him, was not a good thing.

THE IRISH TIMES

24-28 TARA STREET, DUBLIN 2
Tuesday, October 28th, 2014
irishtimes.com

Pope Francis and the synod

Sir, – Dr Damian O'Maonaigh (October 23rd) claims that the *Humanae Vitae* ideal has been left untried because it is difficult. It is fortunate that this is so. Had it become the arbiter of life then typical family sizes, particularly in the West, would be very much larger than they are. This would be bad for the planet, which is already overpopulated.

It would be bad for individual countries. They would find, like Ireland in the 1950s and the Philippines today, that people would become their biggest export. Above all, it would be bad for women, who would be reduced to the status of brood mares.

That women manifestly do not want this state of affairs is amply attested to by the fact that they have, wherever it is possible for them to do so, embraced the empowerment to limit family size that is afforded by modern methods of contraception.

This includes, in general, those women who profess adherence to Catholicism. – Yours, etc,
   SEAMUS McKENNA,
   Windy Arbour,
   Dublin 14.

Glorification of violence

In May 1996 a report appeared in the Irish Times about a speech that Dustin Hoffman had given at the 49th Cannes Film Festival, in which he criticised the level of violence in movies and on TV. The actor was quoted as saying that "Commerce and violence are mixed together now in a way like I've never seen before in my lifetime."

The report said that Hoffman drew a connection between film and video violence and massacres in Port Arthur, Australia, and in Dunblane, Scotland, in the same year. He echoed comments made by the Irish film censor, Mr Sheamus Smith, when he rejected the violent US film From Dusk till Dawn.

In Ireland now, according to the Irish Film Censor's Office (IFCO) only the 2014 remake of From Dusk till Dawn as a TV series is classified. Various episodes are rated as suitable for either 15 and over or 18 and over. The 1996 film is available to purchase as a download on YouTube, and there is no mention of it on the Irish Film Censor's Office (IFCO) website.

According to a BBC News report of 2010, the Dunblane shooting led to strict controls over firearms in the UK which, among other things, made it illegal to buy or possess a handgun. These changes were credited with making mass shootings in the UK "extremely rare". Similarly, the Port Arthur massacre led to fundamental changes to Australia's gun laws.

On May 18th 1996 Robert Dunlop had a letter in the Irish Times under the heading "Glorification of violence". He agreed with Dustin Hoffman, and I had some sympathy for their argument as I read the letter, particularly as I had heard a high-ranking Garda say that, in his experience, criminals in Ireland were often influenced by films and TV in the way they handled their guns. Then I got to Mr. Dunlop's suggestion that the Judeo-Christian ethic could be of assistance in reversing the perceived trend towards more violence in society. I had to respond.

My address on this letter to the Irish Times shows I was then living in Donegal, having obtained my divorce and married Marilyn. I was starting to live a normal life, as a Technical Officer with the

Industrial Development Authority (IDA). I was having experiences such as described in the following vignette, but I still found time to write letters to the paper.

The Airport

"He'll have to go around again."

The speaker knew what he was talking about. He was a farmer who owned a piece of land that had a preternatural field. It contained a section so flat, so level, so solid, and so long, that it made a perfect landing strip for light aircraft. He was there because I had phoned him to tell him to herd his cattle off the 'runway'. Our client, an American industrialist, was being brought here as part of an itinerary that would determine where, if at all, he would set up his government grant-aided enterprise.

The pilot offered the plane to the landing strip and then did indeed decide to put on power and go around again. The second time he made a proper approach. They landed, and taxied to a halt.

"Jesus," said my colleague from head office, when he disembarked, "that was a hairy landing."

He had joined me, whose job it was to guide them to meetings with the Chamber of Commerce, the County Council, bankers, and whatever other local notables we could fit in.

"Our client is a nice guy," he said much later, when the Americans had gone to bed after a fine dinner, and we were finishing off the Midleton Very Rare with which we had been plying them. "When we got on the plane to come out here he said he'd been travelling all day and was looking forward to landing at the airport so he could have a shower. I kept quiet. After the aborted landing, and after he had experienced the cow shit that was thrown up on the windows by the wheels, he was probably not too surprised to find that there wasn't even a hut at the 'airport'. But he said nothing."

My work

As Technical Officer I had the opportunity to meet industrialists from many lands, but the majority came from the USA. It was very interesting work, and it tallied well with my interest in, and love of, engineering and all things technical. We had business people who were in the business of making parts for cars, utility vehicles for farmers and construction workers, medical devices (where I got to see my first nuclear reactor, which was used for the sterilisation of the finished product), Fine China dinnerware, clothing such as shirts and what we knew as "women's outerwear".

My job involved first of all assuring the people concerned that, yes, there was no trouble at all in providing you with X million gallons of water a day, or as many gigawatts of high voltage electricity as needed; whatever was required. Then we had to persuade the water and electricity companies to provide these amenities.

At the other end of the scale were the farm gate makers, the small pottery outfits, the potato farmer who wanted to start a French Fries factory.

We got tremendous respect from the ordinary people of Donegal, and from the executives and others in the County Council. We were seen as members of an organisation that could bring prosperity. It helped enormously, of course, that the people of Donegal are famous for their friendliness. In the words of the song,

"Oh, your hearts are like your mountains, in the Hills of Donegal."

THE IRISH TIMES

13 D'OLIER STREET, DUBLIN 2
MONDAY, MAY 27, 1996

GLORIFICATION OF VIOLENCE

Sir, — It might be true that violent movies lead to violent acts on our streets, as implied by Robert Dunlop in your letters page (May 18th). Or it might not. In any event Mr Dunlop's objective of starting a debate on the topic is a worthy one.

The mind boggles, however, at his suggestion that the Judaeo-Christian ethic can be of assistance in reversing the perceived trend towards more violence in society. This is a tradition that is predicated on violence. In our schools, young children are invited to dwell on every smallest detail of the execution of a man through his being suspended on a specially constructed device by means of nails driven through his limbs. His death was used for centuries, in its turn, as a justification for the insidious violence of anti-Semitism. The idea was, as enunciated to this writer by his primary school teacher in the 1950s, that the Jews "were condemned to wander the earth because they crucified Our Lord".

In history, we have had the Crusades, where countless thousands of innocent men, women and children were brutally put to death; the institutionalised torture of the Spanish Inquisition; the routine and officially sanctioned burning alive of "heretics"; Oliver Cromwell opining that "God will be pleased" at the handiwork of his troops in the cities of Limerick and Drogheda. There is now the situation in Northern Ireland which has, by the most generous analysis, been exacerbated by the refusal of various church authorities to countenance integrated education. The same page that contained Mr Dunlop's letter had another one deploring the violence done to young males by circumcision, another Judaeo-Christian speciality.

We seem to have only very recently ended an era where one particular branch of the Judaeo-Christian tradition, the Roman Catholic Church, presided over a system of public education where brutality and violence were used as tools of instruction. Very obvious psychopaths were given free rein over children in the name of education, including religious instruction. In the process whole generations were given the clear message that violence was a legitimate means to achieve any objective, and it could even be practised on the youngest and most vulnerable members of society.

A screenplay by Vincent Tarantino would not make a good blueprint of how society might be ordered. However, on the evidence of history to date, it might just be preferable to using the Judaeo-Christian example of how things should be done. — Yours, etc.,

SEAMUS McKENNA,
Findrum,
Convoy, Co Donegal.

'Aggressive secularism'

Fintan O'Toole had an opinion piece in the Irish Times in March 2007, where he attacked, with some vigour, the intellectual shortcomings of the then Taoiseach, Bertie Ahern, with regard to his understanding of what republicanism was all about. As well as being Prime Minister, Mr. Ahern was also at the time the leader of Fianna Fáil, the party that liked to style itself The Republican Party.

O'Toole wrote:

> "Nowhere is the intellectual barrenness of Irish politics more obvious than in the absence of even a minimal understanding of the history and meaning of the republican ideal to which all of our largest political parties subscribe.
>
> In the debate sparked by the Taoiseach's recent attack on 'aggressive secularism', the one thing that is clear is that a lot of people, including the Taoiseach, don't get one of the key concepts of republican democracy - what Thomas Jefferson called the "wall of separation between church and state". What they don't get is that the wall was built, not to keep religious people out of public life, but to protect the freedom of conscience of all citizens."

He accused the Taoiseach of setting up a straw man, an abstract concept that has no meaning, in order to tear it down again in support of a spurious argument. He had more to say about Ahern's knowledge of history as well as his flawed understanding of the republican ideal:

> "The United Irishmen, of whom the Taoiseach may have vaguely heard, struggled for a republic in which citizenship, not religion, would be the basis of a person's rights. This indifference is at the core of republican democracy."

The comment about The [Society of] United Irishmen was heavy sarcasm on the part of O'Toole; Ahern's party, Fianna Fáil, has claimed descent, on many occasions, from that august body. It was formed in 1791, a short few years after the French Revolution, which itself is regarded as dating from 1789, the year of the storming of the Bastille in Paris.

The United Irishmen represented all that would be regarded as laudable by those who object to sectarianism, or the dominance in government of those of a particular religion, or rule by a hereditary monarchy. They wanted rule by representative government, which has since come to pass. Their founders were Presbyterians from Belfast. This carries all kinds of irony in the Ireland that existed up to, and immediately after, the creation of Northern Ireland and the foundation of the Irish Republic. This is because this last was dominated in its early years by the dictates of Roman Catholicism, mirrored up north by the existence of a Protestant Unionist government, which did everything it could to deprive Catholic citizens of their civil rights. Many of the foremost proponents of unionism were, and are, themselves Presbyterian.

In the infamous words of Northern Ireland's first Prime Minister, James Craig, the Stormont (Northern Ireland) parliament would be a 'Protestant parliament for a Protestant people.'

The British government suppressed the Society of United Irishmen after they instigated the Irish Rebellion of 1798. There were other consequences too: the hitherto separate, but subservient, Irish Parliament was abolished, and Ireland was incorporated into what became known as The United Kingdom of Great Britian and Ireland, today The United Kingdom of Great Britain and Northern Ireland. This came about as a result of The Act of Union, which came into effect in 1800.

The Irish Parliament sat in the building that later became the headquarters of the Bank of Ireland, in College Green in Dublin, just across the road from Trinity College, Dublin, the single college university that also has a history that adds a great deal to the story of Ireland as a whole.

I sent in the following response to Fintan O'Toole's article.

THE IRISH TIMES
24-28 Tara Street, Dublin 2
Saturday, March 17th, 2007

Providing a real republic

Madam, – Under the above heading, Fintan O'Toole (Opinion, March 13th) provided the most important document to grace the pages of any Irish newspaper for a long time.

It should be reprinted as a pamphlet and sent to every home in the land. It should be read at prime time on all television stations. Above all, in their own interests, it should be carefully studied by the leaders and members of all religious groups and political parties in the land.

It contains wisdom distilled from history's most enlightened thinkers and then – how fortunate we are – served up to us by someone who combines great writing skill with remarkable incisiveness. – Yours, etc,
SEAMUS McKENNA,
Farrenboley Park,
Windy Arbour,
Dublin 14.

But the push to remove religious coercion from the public sphere continued apace.

John Waters debated Christopher Hitchens in the Gate Theatre in Dublin on June 17th 2007. I was in the audience. The debate took place on the stage of the theatre on a Sunday, when the play then running, Sweeney Todd, which told the story of a murderous barber who specialised in spreading flesh, gore and severed heads about the place, was having a night off. The reporters who covered the event, most notably from The Irish Times, made much of the appropriateness of the set of this play as the backdrop for the debate, which was expected itself to be vigorous and tense, if not exactly bloody.

In the event, of course, I had to believe that Hitch won the argument. The main focus was supposed to be Hitch's then new book, God is Not Great, but the most exciting moment of the evening occurred when someone in the audience challenged the author about his transition from a left-wing intellectual to a supporter of some of the principles of American neoliberalism, including the war in Iraq. It seems that this largely came about after Hitchens was disgusted and even traumatised by the outrages that were the attacks on the World Trade Centre in New York, The pentagon, US military headquarters, and two other locations, on September 11th, 2001, now known to history as 9/11.

At the debate the questioner asked Hitchens why he had abandoned all his cherished beliefs, and did he still consider himself a moral being? The author peered out, claimed he could not see the speaker, and wondered, out loud, was he as irritating as he sounded?

"That's the answer of a scoundrel," was the reply.

Then Hitch seemed to lose it. He pointed his finger in the general direction of his critic and said, loudly:

"Fuck off!, fuck off."

That was the end of that particular line of "debate".

Prior to his discussion on stage with Hitchens, Waters had coined the phrase "aggressive secularism". This was taken up and used by Bertie Ahern in some of his public pronouncements, a fact alluded to by O'Toole in his article.

THE IRISH TIMES

24-28 Tara Street, Dublin 2

TUESDAY MARCH 7TH 2007

Madam, – Contrary to what John Waters, or Bertie Ahern's speechwriters, might think, it is not a goal of secularism to denigrate religion.

A truly secular society would guarantee freedom of religion, which also means freedom *from* religion. Freedom for all taxpayers to send their children to schools run and paid for by the State where they would not be isolated by the so-called ethos of the school. If there is to be an ethos in State schools it should consist of respect for the civic duties that make people good citizens. It should encompass equal treatment of all citizens.

This is most certainly not achieved by making the sons and daughters of secularists, humanists, agnostics and, yes, even atheists, sit apart when all other pupils are being taught the principles of one particular religion which, because of an accident of history, happens to conform to the "ethos". – Yours, etc,

SEAMUS McKENNA,
Farrenboley Park,
Dublin 14.

THE IRISH TIMES

Letters

'Anti-Christian' secularism

Thu May 10 2012

Sir, – Nobody can enter the secularism debate, it would seem, without having to face being labelled militant or accused of suppressing freedom of expression, among other things (May 9th).

Secularism is about fairness. At the moment, those who espouse the religious viewpoint occupy an inequitable position in our State-funded schools.

Over 90 per cent of them are managed by religious organisations that have free rein to indoctrinate (and lest people object to this terminology, I have to ask what else would anyone do with religious doctrine?) our children while their intellects are still in formation and their critical faculties have not been developed.

This is wrong and it would be equally wrong if such a facility were provided to even one atheist group.

I don't know of any pro-choice activist who would prevent people opposing their viewpoint, and if such a demand were to be made it would be outrageous. However, an absolute ban on abortion, which disallows even the most early-stage termination under any and all circumstances, is indeed driven by religious doctrine.

If its advocates want to claim something else, then they have to be prepared to be accused of being, at best, disingenuous. – Yours, etc,

SEAMUS McKENNA,
Farrenboley Park,
Windy Arbour,
Dublin 14.

We had the novel display of two priests having a public spat about Catholic teaching. I found this very interesting in view of my early experience of the church. For me it had always been a monolithic, highly disciplined organisation.

The nub of the matter is the fact that, during the time that the precepts that the two priests were arguing about were commonly accepted in the parishes and, by extension, in the schools, they were regarded as infallible truths, and anyone who stepped away from them, in word or deed, was likely to be severely punished. Remember, we all had to go to confession and report to a man who was, at best, known to us from a distance, the actions we had indulged in in the privacy of our own bedrooms, whether alone or with others.

The question of masturbation, particularly male masturbation, is a good case in point. Nowadays, when I read personal advice columns, where the question of when and how a parent should start to talk to their offspring about achieving orgasm on one's own, and the therapeutic effects of such practice, I shudder at the lengths to which priests went to convince teenagers that they were committing one of the most heinous crimes known to man if they were to even think about something that would lead to ejaculation.

It was that bad. The levels of guilt that were engendered, particularly in young people of a sensitive nature, who were trusting of the instruction that was given to them by adults, especially those in positions of authority, were high indeed.

Male masturbation was regarded as far more serious than female masturbation. I now understand that this had its origin the early church belief that the soul originated in the male. It became real, according to this early confusion of the manner in which fertilisation takes place, when at conception the sperm entered the egg. Therefore, to waste sperm was to commit grave sin. The belief also points up the ease with which the early church could accommodate misogyny; female masturbation was not serious as no sperm was 'wasted'. Never mind the fact that, in males, sperm becomes useless after a short time, and are continuously being reproduced in the body. The excess, useless sperm are either subsumed back into the system, or are expelled in nocturnal emissions; what we used to call wet dreams.

THE IRISH TIMES

Letters   17th January 2008

Conscience and Catholic Church

Madam, - The debate in your Letters page between Frs Twomey and Fagan is an interesting development for those of us who grew up under the burden of traditional Catholicism in Ireland. Two Catholic priests are debating openly and, in so doing, are providing an insight to the processes that shaped the repression we endured in the middle decades of the last century and which, in turn, I would venture, motivates many of the people who post on the website www.atheist.ie.

Fr Twomey points out that certain things that people were told by the church were never authoritative church teachings. They were promulgated by individual theologians and based on false assumptions. The tragedy, of course, is that throughout history that did not stop them having the power to dominate people's lives.

To hear now that they were "disputed questions" in the exalted realms of theology, knowing that they were beaten into children by their parents and local clergy, and held to be applicable to adults under the reprehensible psychological threat of eternal damnation, is more than a little hard to take.

Frs Twomey and Fagan are, of course, to be thanked for allowing the fresh air of public debate to blow about these issues. That one may feel it necessary to give thanks for this is a measure of the singularity of such a development among those who are, after all, officers in that bastion of obfuscation, the Catholic Church of Rome.

- Yours, etc,

SEAMUS McKENNA, Farrenboley Park, Windy Arbour, Dublin 14.

Religious symbols in public places

The separation of church and state extends to more than education, health, and reproductive rights, of course. In 2014, the members of Kerry Co. Council decided to put a crucifix in their newly revamped meeting chamber. I saw this as a negation of what, to me, was the republican principle that religion should not be forced on those who wished to operate in the public sphere, perhaps by putting themselves forward for election to a county council, and I said so.

THE IRISH TIMES

24-28 TARA STREET, DUBLIN 2
Tuesday, June 10th, 2014
irishtimes.com

Religious symbol in council chamber

Sir, – Councillors in Kerry who have insisted on placing a religious symbol in the revamped council chambers in Tralee are acting unwisely because they are inviting those who might reject such a move to explain their objections ("Crucifix erected in Kerry County Council meeting chamber", June 6th).

This is likely to be interpreted by the supporters of the symbolism as yet another "attack on religion" when it will be, in fact, nothing more than fair comment.

A great many people who are happy to observe and practice their religious beliefs in private and with dignity will have them held up to ridicule, and will be once more confronted with the detail of how the same beliefs have been betrayed by those who set themselves up as leaders of religion in the past.

Whatever the councillors of Kerry might think, religion should be a personal matter. If they are acting out of pure conviction, one has to ask how sure can they be of their beliefs if they need to have them reinforced by such public display. If this is a populist measure, it is beneath contempt. – Yours, etc,
SEAMUS McKENNA,
Farrenboley Park,
Dublin 14.

The teaching of science

In October 2014 the Irish Times published a thoughtful and detailed letter from David McConnell in support of the Humanist tradition. His point was that very many decent people, who believe in the rule of law and in compassion towards living things, are well able to get on with their lives without the beliefs that religious adherence requires, such as a God, an immortal soul, life after death, transubstantiation, the virgin birth, the Trinity, resurrection from the dead, and the authority of the church. I was delighted to be able to back up his contribution with the following offering:

THE IRISH TIMES

24-28 TARA STREET, DUBLIN 2
Tuesday, October 14th, 2014
irishtimes.com

Science and religion

Sir, – Thanks to David McConnell for a comprehensive and thoughtful contribution to the debate on belief. While I applaud all of the points he makes, the most important for me is his assertion that it is not fair for those who believe in God to insist that this belief should intrude into the lives of those who do not.

This is at the core of the difficulties we have experienced here in Ireland for very many years. Non-believers can live with the religiously denominated holidays and the inclusion of religion in the language (nobody has any difficulty with naming certain days of the week after ancient Norse and Germanic gods, after all), but as long as we have religious discrimination in our state-run, taxpayer-funded schools and as long as reproductive medicine continues to be influenced by religious precepts that make no sense to those who simply cannot come to believe in any supernatural explanations for the phenomena that we see around us, we will continue, as a nation, to serve up injustice. – Yours, etc,
SEAMUS McKENNA,
Windy Arbour,
Dublin 14.

John McGahern and religion

In October 2015 I was able to bring the formidable writing talents of John McGahern to bear on the question of religion. He was no longer with us at this time but he had spoken to us, if you like, from beyond the grave, in an article he contributed to Granta magazine.

In that piece McGahern wrote that his attitude to religious belief was along the lines laid out by Sigmund Freud in his short book, The Future of an Illusion. In it Freud wrote:

> "Let us try gauging the dogmas of religion ... When we ask what their claim to be believed is based on, we receive three answers that are oddly out of harmony with one another. Firstly, they are worthy of belief because our forefathers believed in them back then; secondly, we possess proof handed down to us from that same dim and distant time; and thirdly, it is forbidden to ask for such authentication anyway. This kind of undertaking was once punished with the utmost severity, and even today society frowns on anyone trying it again. This third point inevitably arouses our strongest misgivings. There can only ever be one motive for such a ban, namely that society is well aware of the shakiness of the claim it makes for its religious teachings. Otherwise it would surely have no hesitation in providing anyone who wished to form his own conviction with the necessary means."

Sigmund Freud. The Future of an Illusion (p. 26). Penguin Books Ltd. Kindle Edition.

One of Freud's foremost objections to subscribing to religious belief lay in the fact that there had been in the past such condign punishment reserved for those who were unwise enough to articulate their doubts on the matter. Many of them were tied to a stake driven into the ground and then burned, while still alive, until they died. Their loved ones and neighbours were forced to watch while this obscenity was taking place.

THE IRISH TIMES

24-28 TARA STREET, DUBLIN 2
Wednesday, October 14th, 2015
irishtimes.com

Is a new conformism stifling debate?

Sir, – Breda O'Brien ("The norms may have changed but the pressure to conform remains", Opinion & Analysis, October 10th) is correct in identifying a culture of conformism in much of Irish society. Its roots have been established over many generations.

The origin of this feature of being Irish was, I believe, identified by John McGahern in an article in *Granta* magazine in 2006, when he wrote about the ordinary farming people he grew up among who saw "this version of Roman Catholicism as just another ideological habit they were forced to wear like all the others they had worn since the time of the Druids". – Yours, etc,
    SEAMUS McKENNA,
    Windy Arbour, Dublin 14.

The Catholic right wing

St. Patrick's College, Maynooth, has long been the foremost training institution for Catholic priests in Ireland. In 2015 a number of issues arose there which had the effect of making the then Archbishop of Dublin, Diarmuid Martin, decide to stop sending his seminarians, or trainee priests, to Maynooth. Foremost among them was a rumoured "gay subculture" there. Dr. Martin announced he was sending three seminarians to study at the Irish College in Rome instead.

In an article in the Irish Times its Religious Affairs Correspondent, Patsy McGarry, reported that this announcement was welcomed by the Catholic right wing, or the very conservative element in the church, who saw the upset as a chance to reform what they regarded as an ultra-liberal seminary, and to bring back such things as the Latin mass, traditional clerical dress, support for the doctrine of the Real Presence and the divinity of Christ, and the belief that salvation was dependent on faith alone, and not on good works. Transubstantiation was also mentioned.

I saw the list from the Catholic right as being selective. I could not resist the urge to remind readers of some of the other things that made Christianity notorious in the Middle Ages and which, by rights, I believed should be included in any conservative list of requirements.

On reflection, there is one aspect of the early church that has not been lost. I recall seeing Mary McAleese, when she was President of Ireland, giving a speech on TV from a Catholic Church pulpit. I'm paraphrasing here, but I recall her starting her talk by saying something along the lines that she was the first woman to have stood in this pulpit that did not have a cloth and a can of Mister Sheen in her hands. That delighted me. Here was someone standing up for her principles and damn the consequences. Here was someone who was carrying on her criticism to the rank misogyny that has always existed, not only in the Catholic religion, but in many others also, particularly those founded on the teachings of Mahomed.

Ms. McAleese now has another axe to grind: she has articulated total opposition to the church's attitude to gay people. Her beloved son, Justin, came out as a gay man when he was twenty-one. She has put on record the anguish he suffered when he discovered what the church thought of homosexuality. He felt he was being bullied, as indeed he was.

There is also plenty of evidence that the church's stand on homosexuality gives comfort and support to those who would commit acts of violence against gay people. Why should an established religion be exempt from the laws against hate speech?

As a staunch Catholic, who seems to be determined to deal with the issues that bother her about that institution from the inside, Ms. McAleese is on record as saying:

"The Catholic Church's teaching on homosexuality made it 'difficult but not impossible' to be a committed Catholic."

THE IRISH TIMES

24-28 TARA STREET, DUBLIN 2
Tuesday, August 9th, 2016
irishtimes.com

Changing times at Maynooth

Sir, – The schedule of requirements of the Catholic right wing, as articulated by Patsy McGarry ("Why the Catholic right wants a 'cleanout' in Maynooth", August 5th), which includes a commitment to the Real Presence, condemnation of any questioning of the divinity of Christ, the insistence that faith alone is required for salvation and that good works count for nothing (pure Luther, by the way) and the old chestnut of transubstantiation, are no doubt held with devout sincerity by their proponents, but the list is incomplete.

To be full, it would have to include ecclesiastical courts with unbounded powers, examination of heretics with the aid of the rack, and the public burning of same at the stake in those cases where they felt unable to recant. – Yours, etc,
SEAMUS McKENNA,
Dublin.

In June of 2017 Breda O'Brien, a long-time columnist with a Catholic-centred approach to life, but a good heart, wrote a piece that deplored the fact that the Ireland of today, which she sees as 'secular', still fails children. Her thesis was centred on inadequate training for Gardai when they were called upon to deal with crimes involving children, and the fact that progress had been made on the question of abortion in Ireland, which her church, of course, would ban under any and all circumstances.

She used the phrase "shiny secular Ireland".

Certainly, the police, social workers, teachers and those involved in healthcare cannot have enough proper training when it comes to dealing with young people, but I felt that Breda was laying it on a bit thick.

THE IRISH TIMES

24-28 TARA STREET, DUBLIN 2
Tuesday, June 6th, 2017
irishtimes.com

'Shiny, secular Ireland'

Sir, – There is one outstanding difference between the Ireland of Breda O'Brien's parents and the relatively secular society (we have some way to go yet, particularly in our State-funded schools) that exists now. When failures and even the smallest of shortcomings are found in childcare and in other areas involving the vulnerable today, they receive the spotlight of serious publicity as soon as they come to light. In her parents' time, exactly the opposite happened.

Deplorable abuse, on a massive scale, was systematically covered up by all concerned, including the media and various organs of the State, whose members were in thrall to the Catholic Church.

The concept of the protected disclosure would have been totally alien to your columnist's parents. Anyone with the temerity to attempt to be a whistleblower would have been excoriated by both their superiors and their colleagues, as well as by the public at large. – Yours, etc,
SEAMUS McKENNA,
Windy Arbour,
Dublin 14.

Oaths of office, and other swearing

Another aspect of a proper secular state would be the discontinuation of the requirement for religious oaths in relation to certain aspects of life. Successful candidates for the office of the President, for example, are required to do this. It would be very hard to ask someone who finds it impossible to believe in a deity to start their career in office with the words: "I swear to almighty God…". Yet this is precisely what happens. The end result is that people who find themselves in that position must pretend to believe in order to proceed. This is not conducive to integrity and honour.

At least in courts in Ireland now it is possible to affirm when giving evidence, instead of swearing an oath.

I was able to have something printed about this situation in November of 2018. It would also appear that a letter writer took issue with the name of the organisation that represents atheists in Ireland.

THE IRISH TIMES

24-28 TARA STREET, DUBLIN 2
Friday, November 16th, 2018
irishtimes.com

Atheists and the Constitution

Sir, – Those of us who affirm as opposed to swear when required to do so in court, for example, know that we are making a promise to the State to support the rule of law when we undertake to tell the truth. It is also very much the case that the fear of the punishments prescribed for perjury, and the skill of cross-examiners, have been far more important in the past than the involvement of any deity in ensuring that the facts emerge. That would remain the case were oaths to be abolished.

Atheist Ireland, whatever quibbles a letter writer (November 15th) might have with its name, is correct.

Conscientious non-believers should be able to take public office without being obliged to indulge in hypocrisy because of the current requirement that they must solemnly invoke a belief in an esoteric entity to which they emphatically do not subscribe. – Yours, etc,
SEAMUS McKENNA,
Windy Arbour,
Dublin 14.

Then I wrote about the difference between tolerance, on the one hand, and equality on the other. It is an undeniable fact that if Irish schools, the running of which is paid for by the state, including the provision of teachers' salaries, are allowed to call themselves Catholic schools, then it follows that those children of citizens who do not subscribe to the Catholic religion are merely tolerated when it comes to them getting an education. An education to which they are entitled, under the law, and an education which, if their parents were deny them, would bring with it criminal sanction.

The following letter was written as recently as 2021. No progress has been made on this matter since then, and there is little sense out there that something will happen any time soon.

THE IRISH TIMES

24-28 TARA STREET, DUBLIN 2
Saturday, November 20th, 2021
irishtimes.com

Taking God out of oath

Sir, – The European Court of Human Rights judgment ("Shortall to table Bill on taking God out of oath", November 19th) was made on very narrow legal grounds. It does not in the slightest reflect the reality in modern Ireland, just as with the fact that one branch of one particular religion has control of over 90 per cent of our State-funded primary schools, which merely tolerate the children of those who do not subscribe to it.

Non-Catholics who are citizens of the country deserve more than tolerance. They deserve equality. They are entitled to the same freedoms as those who claim adherence to Christianity. Should an agnostic or an atheist become a judge or the president they should not be obliged to swear a solemn oath to a being in the existence of which they have no confident belief. It will be a shameful act if the Government opposes Róisín Shortall's bid to have a referendum on the matter of oaths for State appointments.

– Yours, etc,
SÉAMUS McKENNA,
Windy Arbour,
Dublin 14.

Chapter FOUR

What's the alternative?

When Finn McRedmond, at that stage a fairly new addition to the Irish Times journalistic staff, responsible for opinion pieces, wrote about an alternative to the religious domination that had existed in Ireland for so long, I thought we might be getting somewhere.

I had long been bothered about the well-justified belief that one of the reasons why people are so strongly attached to the idea of religion is that most people need something to hold on to. They need something to which they can give allegiance, and if that something provides social and community supports for them, then so much the better. How do they deal with this matter in other countries?

Thomas Jefferson, the third president of the United States, a founding father, and the man who promulgated the idea of a wall of separation between church and state, was himself a person of deep religious conviction. He also, however, strongly believed that belief in a deity was a personal matter. There should be no established religion in the country, that would dictate a citizen's allegiance, and he and his fellow founding fathers had this principle installed in the Constitution. It's part of the First Amendment, in a section that has become known as The Establishment Clause. It begins:

> "Congress shall make no law respecting an establishment of religion, or prohibiting the free exercise thereof..."

The framers believed that freedom of religion also meant freedom from religion.

The whole question was of great import in the America of the time. It was a new country, and various religious groupings were struggling for domination. Foremost among them, and the ones that could justifiably think that if there was a state religion they would be it, would have been of a protestant hue. One thing was certain, Roman Catholicism would not have been at the races in such a competition. Therefore, the Catholic Church in the USA was a staunch supporter of Jefferson's idea. In fact, it has often been claimed that it was the Establishment Clause that was the most important factor, along with the immigration of large numbers of Catholics from Europe, from such countries as Poland, Italy, and Ireland, that allowed that church to gain such a strong foothold in America.

Contrast this attitude with the domination, in its early years, of the new Irish state by Catholicism. There was a clause in the Irish Constitution that declared that church to have a "special position" in the country. It was as close as you could get to an established religion. The framers of the original Constitution of Ireland took a lot of its ideas from the Constitution of the USA, but the establishment clause was not one of them.

The original *BUNREACHT NA hÉIREANN* contained this clause:

"The State recognises the special position of the Holy Catholic Apostolic and Roman Church as the guardian of the Faith professed by the great majority of the citizens."

That provision of the Irish Constitution was removed by referendum in 1972.

So, Thomas Jefferson and his colleague founding fathers realised the importance of not giving any particular religion a guarantee by the state. There should be a complete separation, in fact. And, at least in the US, there is. So much so that religious groups are forbidden from using state facilities, such as schools, for their activities, even after hours. This rule has been upheld by even the most conservative of Supreme Court justices.

But what, Jefferson and his friends wondered, could take its place?

The third president, and his followers, believed that what should take the place of religion was allegiance to the state, and what should take the place of religious instruction was the teaching of what it meant to be a good citizen.

I sent in the following letter:

THE IRISH TIMES

24-28 TARA STREET, DUBLIN 2
Friday, June 2nd, 2023
irishtimes.com

Ireland and the decline of religion

Sir, – Finn McRedmond searches for an alternative to the authoritarian, reactionary colossus that dominated Ireland for so long, from the influence of which we are only now, and tentatively, extricating ourselves.

But the alternative is already here. It is called republican democracy.

This relies on adherence to, and respect for, the rule of law, the understanding that minorities have rights, and transparency in governance. Instead of inculcating a belief in an imaginary deity with supernatural powers, these are the things we should be presenting to our children in our schools. We should be letting them know that adherence to these values can be demonstrated, in practical ways, to be to their own benefit.

There is no need to rely on mysteries, or blind faith, or arcane ceremonials in order to further progress the trend that has already begun towards a responsible, healthy and caring society. – Yours, etc,

SEAMUS McKENNA,
Dublin 14.

Blasphemy law

Up to 16 January 2020, when the relevant law was repealed, Ireland had laws that allowed people to be prosecuted for what was known as "Blasphemous Libel" or the making of any statements that were offensive to religion. For many years it only applied to Christianity, but in 1999 this element was found to be unconstitutional as it offended against the provision that guaranteed religious equality.

Charlie Hebdo is the name of a French satirical magazine that has a strong attachment to the idea of freedom of expression. This came into savage confrontation with Muslims, who regard any depiction of Muhammed to be a heinous crime. Charlie Hebdo confronted that head-on by putting cartoons of the prophet in its magazine. It had also in the past lampooned Christianity, Judaism, and other groups that might find themselves newsworthy.

On 7 January 2015 the offices of Charlie Hebdo in Paris were attacked by two Muslim brothers who claimed to be part of Al-Qaeda, the organisation that is generally held to be responsible for the 9/11 attacks on the World Trade Centre and other locations in the US. 12 people were killed in Paris that day, and 11 injured. The attackers went on the run but were tracked down and killed by an elite French police unit.

Something called blasphemy was banned by the Constitution of Ireland since the start. It said that "the publication or utterance of blasphemous, seditious, or indecent matter", was banned, and that these were offences "which shall be punishable in accordance with law". The problem was that such matter was not defined. It appears it was up to a court to decide whether or not something was blasphemous. The public understanding of what might be seditious or indecent was always going to evolve. For example, in the early years of the state homosexual acts were regarded as indecent, even when carried out in private, but by 1993, when being gay was decriminalised, that idea had undergone a sea-change in the public consciousness.

By the first decade of the 21st. century it was becoming clear that blasphemy by any definition was not something that the public would tolerate being prosecuted in the courts. Nevertheless the Constitutional ban remained in force, which was an anomaly. Then, in 2009 Dermot Ahern, who was the then Minister for Justice, decided to bring in a law introducing a new offence, the publication or utterance of blasphemous matter. But this still did nothing to assist the courts in the matter of what constituted blasphemy.

Finally, when a new government came in in 2018, a referendum was eventually held on the question. The people of Ireland decided to remove the ban completely, and the legislation to give effect to that was passed in 2020, as mentioned above. But that was some five years after the 'Charlie Hebdo' terror attacks in France. The day after those attacks a Dublin based Muslim cleric announced that he would take legal action under Irish blasphemy legislation were any Irish magazine to carry depictions of Muhammed.

I took exception to that in the following letter.

THE IRISH TIMES

24-28 TARA STREET, DUBLIN 2
Saturday, January 10th, 2015
irishtimes.com

'Charlie Hebdo' shootings and terror attacks in France

Sir, – Your report containing the words of Dr Ali Selim of the Islamic Cultural Centre of Ireland ("Dublin based cleric warns of legal action over religious depictions", January 8th), to the effect that he would be prepared to pursue a legal action under blasphemy legislation if "an Irish media organisation or social media carried a depiction of Muhammad, an act which Muslims find offensive", constitutes the best argument so far for the repeal of this ridiculous legislation.

Even the fact that such a thing can be contemplated here, in the light of the appalling attack on freedom of expression in Paris, a nursery of democratic republicanism, is calculated to earn Ireland the opprobrium of the rest of the developed world, and deservedly so.
– Yours, etc,
SEAMUS McKENNA,
Windy Arbour,
Dublin 14.

Chapter FIVE

Religious control of education in Ireland

Origins and comparisons

In the book "Essays in the History of Irish Education", edited by Brendan Walsh, published by Palgrave Macmillan Limited, 2016, Tom Walsh, in his essay entitled "The national System of Education 1831 – 2000", shows that it was the intention of the framers of the Irish education system in 1831 that education should be interdenominational as regards religion. Similarly, in 2010, Garret FitzGerald, a former Taoiseach highly regarded by many, wrote that

> "The original primary school system was envisioned as being interdenominational" (Irish Times article Sat Feb 13 2010: "How religion made its way into the primary school system").

The principle that schools should not force religion on its pupils as the price of getting a general education was enshrined in the Irish Constitution after the foundation of the state. Article 44.4 says:

> Legislation providing State aid for schools shall not ... be such as to as to affect prejudicially the right of any child to attend a

school receiving public money without attending religious instruction at that school.

If you take out the 'shall not' and the 'without', which effectively amount to a double negative, and understand that "affect prejudicially" means "to damage", what the clause says is that a child cannot be forced to attend religious instruction in a school that receives financial aid from the state.

Right since the very start, religious denominations of all sorts have attempted to control the minds of the young through education. Despite the aims of the founders of the education system in Ireland, the Catholic Church, in particular, was so successful in subverting the ideal that all children should be educated together, and religion should be dealt with outside of school hours, that Tom Walsh was able to write:

> "At the Catholic General Synod in Maynooth in 1900, the hierarchy indicated its overall satisfaction with the system being 'as denominational as we could desire'".

In his 2010 article, Garret Fitzgerald distilled the history of the situation we have today in Ireland in the following words:

> "And so, in October 1831, shortly after Catholic Emancipation, chief secretary Edward Stanley, by way of a letter to the Duke of Leinster inviting him to chair a new board of commissioners of national education, founded our national school system. For the next 170 years two variants of that letter (the original of which had been lost) remained the sole basis for the existence of our national schools.
>
> Joint applications for the establishment of interdenominational schools were to be made to this board by the different religious groups in each area. But, while the Catholic hierarchy had accepted this new interdenominational system, it was bitterly opposed, (and within eight years had been comprehensively sabotaged) by

the Protestant religious authorities, who refused to join in making joint applications. In 1839 the Presbyterians secured changes in the rules which gave a strong denominational complexion to their schools, and in the same year the Church of Ireland created its own separate organisation to run its schools: the Church Education Society.

The board, clearly anxious not to disappoint the Catholic community, felt it had no choice but to accept applications coming from one denomination only, and so a de facto Catholic national school system came into existence, with the bishops as school patrons in each diocese, ensuring that the teachers in their schools were Catholics.

I emphasise the words "de facto denominational". For the principle that all schools remained open to children of all denominations survived, as did the principle that no children could be required to attend denominational religious instruction. The latter principle was, indeed, incorporated in both the 1922 constitution (Article 8) and that of 1937 (Article 44.4).

However, in August 1932 two provisions relating to primary education were dropped, in recognition of the fact that they had long ceased to apply. *These had been that as far as possible children of all persuasions would be educated in the same schools, and that the clergy and laity of different religious denominations should co-operate in conducting national schools".* (my emphasis, SMcK) Nevertheless, in the Irish Free State religious instruction remained separate from the rest of the curriculum, being provided normally between 12 to 12.30 so as to facilitate the withdrawal of non-Catholic children – thus safeguarding the constitutional rights of minority participants in the system.

The really fundamental switch to an avowedly denominational school structure came much later, in January 1965, through a little-noticed change by the Department of

Education in the national school rules, which was authorised by the then minister Paddy Hillery.

On the basis of a reference in Article 44.4 to "schools under the management of different religious denominations" these new rules declared that the State "gives explicit recognition to the denominational character of primary schools".

Drawing on this assertion, in 1971 the Department of Education, under Padraic Faulkner, issued new rules for primary education based, "on the following theses . . . that the separation of religious and secular instruction into differentiated subject compartments, [which had been a key element of the system since its inception] serves only to throw the whole educational function out of focus". Thenceforth, religion was to permeate the whole curriculum."

This, then, is the origin of the so-called integrated curriculum, where Catholic religious principles are made to permeate all subjects in the school, and where pupils of all religions and none are exposed to Catholic imagery in the common areas of the school. I started writing to the editor of the Irish Times on the subject of the separation of church and state in education in Ireland at an early stage. Here's one of the first:

THE IRISH TIMES
24-28 Tara Street, Dublin 2
Tuesday, Septemmber 25, 2007

Madam, – Niall O'Donoghue's evaluation of the secular school system in Finland (September 22nd) is apt. The same model, which excludes all religious involvement in state schools, is in use in France and the US.

If it can serve these two substantially if not perfectly integrated societies, with a combined population of 361 million people, it can also work well here in Ireland. – Yours, etc,

SEAMUS McKENNA,
Farrenboley Park,
Windy Arbour,
Dublin 14.

The church goes legal

I had a letter in the paper, in December of 2015, alluding to one of the Department of Education rules of 1971 (rule 68), mentioned by Garret FitzGerald in his article above (see p. 52).

A report had appeared in The Irish Times of Dec 09 2015. This confirmed for me that the Catholic Church in particular, but also the other Christian churches, had subverted the principle that taxpayers' money should not be used to benefit any one grouping, but rather all citizens, especially when it comes to education. Here's a quote:

> "'It is not the role of the Minister to determine or interfere with the ethos of faith schools. Legal advice available to the Department of Education confirms this,' it [*The Bishops' Council for Education*] said."

THE IRISH TIMES

24-28 TARA STREET, DUBLIN 2
Friday, December 11th, 2015
irishtimes.com

Primary religion classes and rule 68

Sir, – They may believe they have a legal opinion on their side, which is very far from being a binding judgment, but Catholic bishops have some nerve in telling the Minister for Education, an elected representative, that she does not have a role in the admission and curriculum policies (covered in this case by the odious term "ethos") of schools that are funded by the same state, and by extension by all of its citizens ("Bishops tell minister not to 'interfere' in schools", December 10th).

The vast majority of our state schools are now being described by apologists for the current grossly inequitable arrangements as "faith schools". It is incomprehensible how such things could exist in a modern democratic state unless they are funded in their entirety by the religious denomination that created them. This is very far from being the case in relation to the schools in question. – Yours, etc,
SEAMUS McKENNA,
Windy Arbour, Dublin 14.

A few weeks later Fintan O'Toole wrote a piece that called for more state involvement in primary education. This idea was challenged by Seamus Mulconry, who later became Secretary General of the Catholic Primary Schools Management Association. I, in turn, took issue with him. The following was the result:

THE IRISH TIMES

Trusted journalism since 1859

24-28 Tara Street, Dublin 2
Thursday, December 27th, 2007

State, church and primary schools

Madam, — Seamus Mulconry castigates Fintan O'Toole for advocating more state involvement in primary education. This Thatcherite reflex would be fine and laudable if primary education were a business segment, where competition could temper the behavior of participants and lead, via closures and amalgamations, to maximum efficiency. But primary education is not a business. It is, in fact, one of the best examples of an activity where it is far more important to be effective than it is to be efficient.

Effective at what? What should be the goals of primary education? They should not, I submit, include the promotion of adherence to the tenets of any religion. That function belongs in the home and in the church, mosque, or synagogue. Primary schooling should be about grounding in the requirements of literacy and numeracy, but also in the imparting of what it means to be a good citizen. Only the state can do this properly. Only the state can educate the young people of the country fairly and impartially. Only the state can ensure the enrolment of pupils according to criteria that do not leave some behind because of the religion they happen to be born into.

This has not happened a lot in this country, but the fact that it has happened at all to even a small minority of children, is a disgrace so large that it cries out for the current system of primary school patronage to be abolished. Mr. Mulconry's sideswipe at the problems of integration in France is disingenuous. Were it not for the care that the French constitution takes to separate church and state the problems in the *banlieues* would be infinitely greater than they are at present. — Yours, etc.,

SEAMUS McKENNA,
Farrenboley Park,
Dundrum,
Dublin 14.

The state's responsibility to education

2008 started with a letter from me pointing out that the state had a responsibility to see to it that all children were properly educated, and not only the children of parents who valued education. The plain fact was, I felt, that the children of parents, and there are more than a few, who did not value education were in danger of not being properly treated.

Too many people have grown up in the grip of a cycle of poverty and deprivation which is exacerbated by a lack of respect for learning. Often, parents are themselves disaffected by their own experiences in the educational space, and neglect their children's needs in this regard as a result.

Once again, we come back to the Irish Constitution. It states that parents are the ones who have the primary responsibility for the education of their children. The Catholic Church has fastened on to that to argue that if parents wish to outsource this duty to the church, in the event that they are not qualified to directly instruct their offspring themselves, then they are entitled to do so. Nobody would argue with that, if the church's motivation was benevolent or philanthropic. But it is not. It is self-serving in its desire to maintain or to increase the number of its adherents. In this is was greatly facilitated by the fact that it had gained such influence with political leaders of all stripes at the time of the foundation of the Irish state.

All of that is, pardon the pun, of academic interest to those who are not motivated to learn, either by their parents or by the society in which they find themselves. They need special assistance, and this can only be provided by the state. Words in the Constitution, or in the laws of the land, will have no bearing at all on this tragedy. More practical measures are needed, and resources must be provided to that people do not slip through the net into the perpetual motion machine of early school leaving, dead-end jobs or, which is worse, criminality, and the passing on, to their children, of the attitudes that give rise to this disaster.

THE IRISH TIMES

Letters

Parents' right to educate their children and the constitution

Thu Jan 03 2008 - 00:00

Madam, - Just because the Constitution places the primary responsibility for the education of children on parents does not mean it is necessarily a good idea. What has been happening in practice is that those parents who value education do not need to be reminded of their duty in this regard, to the extent that they will spend large amounts on private education even where excellent free schools are available. On the other hand it has been necessary, in the case of some parents who do not value education, to have the so-called responsibility taken over by the State anyway.

The part of the Constitution giving effect to parental responsibility in education (Article 42) is closely related to that (Article 41) which makes the family the primary "unit group of Society". This has been found wanting to such as extent that the Government is forced to hold a referendum later this year to provide for the rights of children. Would that we had made our primary education system child-centred rather than faith-centred. If we did, we would teach our young people how to think, not what to think.

- Yours, etc,

SEAMUS McKENNA, Farrenboley Park, Dublin 14.

Forum on school patronage

In 2011, when Ruairí Quinn of the Labour Party, which this writer would have thought might have something of a liberal agenda, was Minister for Education, it was announced that there was to be a forum on school patronage.

We had high hopes for Mr. Quinn and his Labour Party, those of us who espoused the ideal of a separation of church and state in education. Apart from the forum on school patronage, the same minister went on to work towards the removal of primary schools from religious patronage, and instead allow other organisations, such as Educate Together, "an independent NGO that runs and supports schools that guarantee equality of access and esteem to children, irrespective of their social, cultural or religious background", to manage them.

According to its website, "Educate Together schools are learner centred in their approach to education and are run as participatory democracies, with respectful partnership between parents, pupils and teachers."

In the event, that initiative turned out to be something far less than a resounding success. A very small number of schools have been "divested" at the time of writing this book, and the accommodation provided for those that have been divested is often of a poor standard.

I have always felt that one of the great problems in relation to education is the fact that the country never got away from the so-called patronage system of education provision. This is where the function of education is delegated by the government to religious groupings. As we have seen, it has its origins in the attitude that prevailed in government when education for the masses was a novel idea. The religions saw this as something that would benefit them, so they put pressure on the political powers-that-be to ensure the they had control of it.

Then the question of secularism came up. Mr. Quinn was quick to point out that the Labour Party did not have a "secular agenda", as if such as thing was something of which to be ashamed. The ideals of republican democracy, as espoused by those who set up the most progressive regimes in history, who gave us the renunciation of hereditary and religious sovereignty in the First and subsequent Republics in France, and in the setting up of the United States of America, with its Constitution and its Bill of Rights, were to be seen as in some way degenerate aspirations. Mr. Quinn should be reminded that Ireland even has the word 'Republic' in its official title.

It has long been apparent to me that the word 'secular' has intimations of atheism for those who would impose religion on all and sundry. The late notorious Archbishop of Dublin, John Charles McQuade, who ruled with an iron fist, albeit with the connivance, apart from a small number of notable exceptions, of the politicians of his day, had as his *bête noire* the rise of Protestantism. It is indeed apparent now that his fears were misdirected; he should have been more concerned with atheism, but not however with secularism. As already noted, secularism was the reason the Catholic Church was not subjugated in the early years of the United States of America. It just seems unfair that it would embrace a liberal principle when it is in its interests to do so, but then reject that same code when it does not need it, in order to dominate its surroundings. The same thing has happened in history with certain deplorable authoritarian regimes; they embraced democracy for as long as they could use it to gain power, but then threw it out completely when they had achieved their dominant position.

My basic point in this and other letters has been that the patronage system itself has, long since, served its purpose. The Department of Education is the body that has the moral responsibility for the treatment of our children during their formative years. It already oversees the payment of all teachers' salaries in the National school system, it regulates and supervises all state examinations, and it pays for the upkeep of schools, at least in principle (that schools are so underfunded that they need to charge parents a ludicrously named 'voluntary contribution' every year is nothing short of a national scandal). It is high time for the government to arrange things so that the same department can take over full management of the schools, and confine the patronage system to the dustbin of history, where it belongs.

THE IRISH TIMES

Letters Thu Mar 17 2011

Changes in school patronage

Madam, – The establishment of a forum on school patronage by the Minister for Education, Ruairí Quinn, is to be welcomed (March 12th).

However, even before it starts, it is disquieting to read that the Minister feels it necessary to deny that the Labour Party has a secular agenda. We must reject the historical mental conditioning that has created the notion that a secular society is in some way an illegitimate aspiration.

A secular State school system, where parents are free to give their children the religious ideas they wish in their homes and in their places of worship, without impinging on the justifiable wishes of those who do not want their children exposed to dogma that is presented as irrefutable fact, is very much to be desired.

A secular agenda is not an atheistic agenda. It simply makes room in the spectrum of belief for those who have no religion. It is nothing short of intolerance that this has not been the case in our State-funded primary schools up to the present time.

The forum on school patronage should have, high up in its terms of reference, the possibility of getting rid of the patronage system altogether and ensuring that our schools are placed directly under the control of the Department of Education. This is what, after a great deal of anguish, we are moving towards in relation to our health system and its supervising government department. – Yours, etc,

SEAMUS McKENNA,
Farrenboley Park,
Windy Arbour, Dublin 14.

The "integrated curriculum"

In January 2013 I wrote in condemnation of the so-called "integrated curriculum". This, the reader will remember, was the provision referenced by Garret FitzGerald in his 2010 Irish Times article "How religion made its way into the primary school system" that pointed out the provisions of "a little-noticed change by the Department of Education in the national school rules".

I remember when I was attending primary school in St. Declan's De La Salle in Waterford, in the 1950s, religious instruction, which I know now was faith formation in Roman Catholicism, was carried out for a half-an-hour each day from 12:30pm to 1:00pm. I have found out also that the reason this particular thirty minutes was chosen was so that pupils of parents who wished their children not to receive such instruction could leave for lunch at half-twelve instead on one o'clock. There was something else as well: the religious classes were always conducted through the medium of English, while all others were done using Irish as the language spoken.

This situation had its origins in the notorious decree of the Irish government run by Eamonn De Valera, which came into power in 1957. This was to the effect that all lessons in state-run schools were to be carried out through the medium of the Irish language (see p 69). They saw this as an experiment in furtherance of the of Irish revival. Imagine. Children's education was to be put at risk for an experiment!

But there was one exception. The notorious, and autocratic, Archbishop John Charles McQuaid was alive to the damage that such a decree might do. He therefore prevailed upon Mr. De Valera to have religious instruction carried out through English. Thus all other subjects could be done using Irish, a language not spoken by the great majority in any situation outside of school, while religious indoctrination was to be carried out using English, the language that the people knew.

The experiment was not a success. Countless young people left school in a state of virtual illiteracy. Not only that, their experience of having Irish "rammed down their throats" in school gave them a lifelong hatred of the language.

THE IRISH TIMES

Letters

Changing school patronage

Fri Jan 11 2013

Sir, – The acknowledgment of the requirement of the EU Convention on Human Rights that parents must have a right to withdraw their children from religious education classes if such classes are not delivered in an "objective, critical and pluralistic manner", by Tom O'Gorman of the Iona Institute (January 8th), places the spotlight squarely on a terrible, long-standing problem.

This is because, in State-funded Irish schools that are under the management of the Catholic Church (over 90 per cent of State schools), it is stated policy that: "This [Catholic] faith is not simply the subject matter of particular lessons but forms the foundation of all that we do and the horizon of all that takes place in the school." (A Vision for Catholic Education in Ireland, issued by the Catholic Bishops Conference, May 2008).

The ultimate logic of this is that parents who demand a secular education for their children are under an obligation to remove them from all classes, and indeed from the school premises, of such taxpayer-funded schools under the current arrangements. This is a shocking indictment of what we like to think is a democratic republic in the 21st century. – Yours, etc,

SEAMUS McKENNA,
Farrenboley Park,
Windy Arbour,
Dublin 14.

Divestment, or the lack of it

As late as January 2014 it was apparent that the divestment of schools by the Catholic Church, so that they could be put under management of a multi-denominational or non-denominational institution, was not happening, despite the promise held out by the Minister of Education (see pages 96 and 97 above).

THE IRISH TIMES

24-28 TARA STREET, DUBLIN 2
Tuesday, September 1st, 2015
irishtimes.com

School patronage and the State

Sir, – Michael Nugent's opinion piece, read in conjunction with the report on the current difficulties around the "divestment" of an isolated, derelict, former Catholic school in Mayo ("Educate Together national school in Mayo fails to open amid row", August 27th), illustrate perfectly the unmanageable, unfair and ultimately downright wasteful nature of the solution that the Government has embarked upon in an effort to provide for pluralism in Irish schools.

The attitude seems to be to do anything to avoid getting rid of the patronage system, no matter how archaic, discriminatory and expensive it is proving to be.

It is time for the authorities to wake up and do their duty by all citizens in this regard and, at the same time, stop wasting taxpayers' money. – Yours, etc,
SEAMUS McKENNA,
Windy Arbour,
Dublin 14.

The next letter probably encapsulates the core argument for the removal of religious influence in Irish state-funded schools. It is one that has not just been made by me but by other contributors, including some on the writing staff of the Irish Times, such as Fintan O'Toole and Joe Humphreys. Other letter writers, like Michael Nugent and Jane Donnelly of Atheist Ireland, and Rob Sadlier of Education Equality, have been making a similar case in the Irish Times letters page for many decades now.

Some years ago the then then Minister for Education, Ruairi Quinn, a former leader of the Labour Party, announced that he had reached an agreement with Catholic and Church of Ireland bishops that would lead to the divestment of schools by the Christian churches, which had the management of more than 90% of state-funded schools, in those areas where there was a demand for secular schooling. That initiative turned out to be a total and absolute failure. I wrote the following, which touched on this, in January of 2014.

It had always intrigued me the way proponents of religion will make claims for religious belief that have nothing whatever to do with the idea that one needs religion in order to be able to do well in the afterlife. In 2014 I found myself dealing with one of these. It was the claim that being imbued with the principles of religion enhances the ability of young people to do well in other subjects, such as the arts and sciences.

Minister for Education, Ruairí Quinn, had suggested, at an Irish Primary Principals' Network meeting, that if more time was needed on the curriculum for literacy and numeracy, then the teacher might look at taking that time from religious education. This shocked the letter writer mentioned in mine below.

It seems to me that a great many people equate education with religious instruction, even today. It goes further; they have it as a core principle that religious instruction is of much more importance that the training of young people in arts and sciences. As long as this situation exists we will struggle to make non-religious education accessible to the people who really need it; the children from those homes where education, of any sort, is not valued by the parents, for whatever reason.

Less religion, more maths?

Sir, – Apart from the fallacy that religious indoctrination enhances literacy and numeracy, Dr Daniel O'Connell (January 29th) must be aware that there are parents who would not have their children in a religious class even if it were to guarantee them a PhD.

At the same time as he made his suggestion that religion should give way to basic literacy and numeracy teaching, the Minister for Education also disclosed that the divestment of schools by religious patrons is simply not happening, despite all the talks and consultations that have taken place. This means that there are still many parents who are in the invidious position of either marking their children as being apart from their peers by extracting them from religious instruction proper, or putting up with them being indoctrinated. This is to say nothing of the injustice that is the integrated curriculum, where religious dogma is presented, unquestioningly, in all other subjects throughout the school day, or the widespread religious iconography in the schools.

It is open to suggestion that those who insist on religious instruction at the expense of basic literacy and numeracy are afraid of the better informed and more rational adults that would result from teachers accepting the Minister's suggestion. – Yours, etc,

SEAMUS McKENNA,
Farrenboley Park,
Windy Arbour,
Dublin 14.

Discrimination in education

Later on that year I got an opportunity to attack what I saw as the unfair system of so-called "voluntary contributions". This is where, in a country where primary education is supposed to be free, schools often need to resort to the practice of seeking monetary contributions from the parents of the pupils in order to cater for ordinary, everyday requirements for their operation. Of course, some parents are better able to afford these contributions than others.

A more insidious note was introduced in certain schools, where it was made plain that, far from being voluntary, parents were obliged to make these payments, as the price of having their children educated.

So we have yet another "Irish solution to an Irish problem." These often come with additional absurdities and contradictions. A good example of the latter is the Equal Status Act 2000. This was brought into being to conform to EU requirements. But all EU legal provisions come with possible derogations. They help to make EU law acceptable to the citizens of particular countries. A good example is the toleration of bull fighting in Spain, an activity that would horrify the citizens of many other countries in the bloc.

According to an Irish government publication, "Schools and the Equal Status Acts, 2nd. Edition", the following are the exceptions to the Equal Status Act 2000:

> **The admission of a student**: A school may not discriminate in relation to the admission of a student to the school, *subject to exemptions set out below* (my emphasis). An exemption applies to the gender ground. Single-sex schools are allowed.
>
> A second exemption concerns schools where the objective is to provide education in an environment that promotes certain religious values. A school that has this objective can admit a student of a particular religious denomination in preference to other students. Such a school can also refuse to admit a student who is not of that religion, provided it can prove that this refusal is essential to maintain the ethos of the school.

It is important to place the second exemption above in context. In Ireland, more that 90% of state-funded schools are under the 'patronage' (read management and control) of Christian religions. This means that a law that has the title "Equal Status", and is ostensibly meant to outlaw discrimination, winds up legalising that very scandal, on religious grounds, in Irish schools! But not just any schools; schools that are funded by the state, and therefore by all taxpayers, those of all religions and none.

THE IRISH TIMES

24-28 TARA STREET, DUBLIN 2
Friday, March 14th, 2014
irishtimes.com

Discrimination in education?

Sir, – The "To Be Honest" writer and Eimear Lynch (March 13) highlight, once again, the absurdity that is the archaic system we in Ireland continue to foist on our children in the name of education.

National school teacher salaries are paid by the State, school buildings are provided by the State and the school inspectorate is under the auspices of the State, as is curriculum development and all other related matters.

The European Court of Human Rights has determined that teachers here are ultimately the responsibility of the State. A solution to the problems of discrimination is thus plain to be seen – we should abolish the patronage system altogether and bring all national schools under the direct management of the Department of Education. A fair and balanced system for school place allocation would follow as a matter of course.

There are other benefits to be gained. For one, the so-called "voluntary" contribution that is demanded of many parents in order for them to secure the right of their children to have a primary education would no longer be an issue.

Of course, whatever shortfall that currently gives rise to this would have to be paid, instead, from the exchequer.

It is not too much to claim, however, that any country that cannot properly fund the education of its young does not deserve to consider itself among the developed nations of the world. – Yours, etc,
SEAMUS McKENNA,
Farrenboley Park,
Windy Arbour,
Dublin 14.

The archaic patronage system in Irish education

The history of national education in Ireland, as detailed by such as Fintan O'Toole and Garret FitGerald, makes it clear that, at the outset, both the culture of the times and the question of who was going to pay for general education meant that the government of the day was pleased to hand over as much as possible of the work required to religious groups. That's how the patronage system for education came into being.

Here in Ireland we missed a perfect opportunity to bring education into the modern world at the foundation of the state. We could have, and should have, made a new start, and put the education of our children directly under the control of the government, through the Department of Education and, at the same time, made it fully child centred.

Unfortunately, we did nothing of the sort. Various ideologues, not merely those of a religious bent, saw defenceless children as the means by which they could propagate their ideas. Nationalists, for example, who saw the Irish language as the means by which they could further their cause, insisted that all subjects should be taught through the medium of Irish in the schools. The government obliged, and made an order to that effect. At the same time all court cases were supposed to be carried out in Irish, the army was to conduct all of its business in a similar manner, and if people called to a government office they were supposed to have their business carried out in the same way.

Our learned friends in the courts were well able to fight their corner, and made short work of those requirements. The Gardai had to continue to investigate crimes through English, as to try to do otherwise would have made their work impossible, and the same went for government offices. The army, to this day, is able to do its work through our native tongue, but the unfortunate children who found themselves having to learn all subjects through the medium of a language that was not spoken in the homes, in the shops, or on the streets, were put into a very difficult situation.

And so it was with religious control of, not only education, but also of health. The religions saw these as the means of maintaining adherence and control.

Later, in an effort to establish plurality in the religious sphere, the government encouraged other groups to become school patrons. My point, in the letter following, was that this opened the door to all kinds of ideologies to attempt to gain control of young people's minds. The only proper solution was to abolish the whole patronage system.

THE IRISH TIMES

24-28 TARA STREET, DUBLIN 2
Thursday, May 15th, 2014
irishtimes.com

National schools and patronage

Sir, – It has to count for something when a law lecturer at NUI Galway declares that the Constitution of Ireland is itself the basis for a range of egregious abuses of human rights in our national school system ("Treatment of non-Catholics urgent human rights issue", Education, May 13th).

Eoin Daly mentions divestment of schools in the context of dealing with the situation. I would go further. I would abolish the so-called patronage system in primary schools altogether, and bring all national schools under the direct control of the Department of Education. They are, after all, funded by all the people through the auspices of the same department.

The patronage system is totally unsuitable for the modern world. Just as religious zealots on a solo run can make a mockery of the efforts of some church people to have inclusion where a religious body has the management of a school, so there is nothing to prevent a teacher with what is to him or her a pressing ideological issue of a more secular nature from indoctrinating young, unformed minds in any school that has a patron other than the State itself. This is because right now there are no standards that would protect our children from any ideology until such time as they are in a position to make judgments themselves on the matters concerned.

One way or the other it is indefensible that the Constitution is being abused in the manner described to deprive one section of the community of its human rights. – Yours, etc,
SEAMUS McKENNA,
Farrenboley Park,
Windy Arbour, Dublin 14.

A sectarian school system?

As 2015 drew to an end I felt it was time to use the term "sectarian" to describe our school system. My contribution that made this charge was printed in the letters page on December 2nd of that year.

THE IRISH TIMES

24-28 TARA STREET, DUBLIN 2
Wednesday, December 2nd, 2015
irishtimes.com

A sectarian schools system?

Sir, – Quite apart from the cost involved, which is itself a serious consideration, the logistical and regulatory compliance issues involved in large infrastructural projects make the oft-repeated mantra of those who would retain religious patronage in our national school system – that the answer to oversubscription in certain areas is "to build more schools" – a trite observation.

Even in those cases where unbaptised children are accepted into the vast majority of our national schools, they are still open to religious indoctrination against the wishes of their parents. This happens because of the so-called "integrated curriculum", which means that Catholic dogma runs through all subjects that are taught in the schools.

In a very real sense, people who find it impossible to subscribe to the idea that there exists a superior, supernatural being that directs matters here on Earth, and who are honest about it, are regarded as second-class citizens in Ireland – a country that has the effrontery to call itself a republic.

A blatantly sectarian schools system? It most certainly is. – Yours, etc,
SEAMUS McKENNA,
Windy Arbour, Dublin 14.

On the morning of Monday, September 19th 2016, I opened the Irish Times to see a letter from Seamus Conboy, Primary Support Officer of Education and Training Boards Ireland. This I read with great interest. It described a formula for handing religion in his schools that I thought would be wonderful if only it could be applied in all schools in the country.

Mr. Conboy's letter is so important I have reproduced it in full here.

Letters to the Editor

Community national schools and faith

Sir, – Catherine O'Brien (September 10th) asks some valid questions of the community national school model. She claims that it is time for some answers, and I couldn't agree more. I hope the fact that the community national schools are now moving formally under the patronage of the Education and Training Boards will mean that the general public will be much better informed about these schools.

Ms O'Brien questions the practices around holy communion and confirmation in particular, so I will focus only on these in this letter.

First, it is important to note that facilitating rites of passage for any child is in response to parental requests for support in this area. As we serve the needs of the community, we are happy to respond to such requests and work with all of our religious and belief communities on this. In my former school, which is currently only up to third class, parents who want their children to make their holy communion are given an option for their child to opt out of one Goodness Me, Goodness You lesson per week. During this lesson, the rest of the class continues with its normal Goodness Me, Goodness You lesson with their class teacher, and the Catholic children are taught more explicit content about the sacrament by one of the infant teachers whose children have already gone home. This arrangement is available to parents from any belief group who wish for the school to facilitate some work around specific rites of passage or celebrations.

It is also important to note that community national

Continued…

...continued.

schools do not provide "sacramental preparation" in the form given to children in Catholic denominational schools. We work with the parents and parish to support the families by providing "sacramental education". It is up to the parents and parish to "prepare" their children for the communion day, and the only aspect we can support is in deepening the child's understanding of the sacrament. Again, this is only during Goodness Me, Goodness You time once per week, and no curricular time is given over to this.

In May this year, we had our first group of children making their holy communion. The success criteria for me was that the Catholic children understood the meaning behind their special day and also that no other child of any other faith or belief felt disadvantaged by the support given to these children.

The children made their communion during a normal Sunday Mass, along with Catholic children from Citywest Educate Together, who we work closely with. I was delighted that so many families from other belief groups came to the school after the Mass and brought food and drinks to contribute to the celebration.

On talking to these parents, many said that they were delighted to do so as they felt their faith and belief was so well-acknowledged and supported by the school, and that the Catholic families always made an effort to join in their own particular celebrations. – Yours, etc,
SÉAMUS CONBOY,
Primary Support Officer,
Education and Training
Boards Ireland,
Naas, Co Kildare.

I would have liked to see the arrangements described by Mr. Conboy made official policy for all taxpayer funded schools, which is a long way from having them practiced in the Educational and Training Board centres of learning, for the reason that they comprise of a relatively small subset of all the schools in the country.

I did welcome his letter on the subject, even if I felt the need to keep the pressure on to have a truly secular education system:

THE IRISH TIMES

24-28 TARA STREET, DUBLIN 2
Thursday, September 22nd, 2016
irishtimes.com

Religion and schools

Sir, – The letter from Séamus Conboy (September 19th) of the Education and Training Boards Ireland (ETBI) seems to describe a decent attempt at squaring the circle of faith formation and the needs of non-believers for their children in our schools. But despite the best efforts of the ETBI there remain very serious problems, amounting to shameful religious discrimination, in State-run schools in Ireland. A major one was highlighted last week by Rob Sadlier (September 15th), who pointed out that the so-called "integrated curriculum" can and does discriminate against parents and children on religious grounds, and in certain cases results in the indoctrination of children against the wishes of their parents.

If the system outlined by Mr Conboy were enshrined in law and made applicable to all State-funded schools across the board, regardless of background of their patrons, then we would be getting somewhere in this matter. In the meantime, we operate a religiously discriminatory State school system, paid for by taxpayers, for which we have been roundly condemned by a number of human rights committees of the United Nations. – Yours, etc,
SEAMUS McKENNA,
Windy Arbour
Dublin 14.

The baptism barrier

It was hard to credit that whether or not one's child had a certificate to confirm that they had been baptised into the Catholic religion would determine where, or even if, they could get a state-funded education in Ireland. But this was the case up to 2018, when the government passed legislation that removed the right of state schools under the "patronage" of the Catholic Church to discriminate on the basis of religion in their admission policies.

As late as 2023 The Catholic Education Partnership was arguing that the removal of the baptism barrier was a "discriminatory law, solely directed at Catholics, and no other faiths" (Irish Times article of Wed Jan 04 2023).

What I found to be particularly hard to take was the determination of the people in charge of the school system, which is funded by all taxpayers, to regard it as being made up of 'their' schools. And the Catholic Church calling anything discriminatory, given its record in this regard, was a bit rich.

THE IRISH TIMES

24-28 TARA STREET, DUBLIN 2
Thursday, February 9th, 2017
irishtimes.com

'Baptism barrier' and schools

Sir, – The topic exercising the minds of all right-thinking people in the developed world at present is whether or not a religious test has been applied to the right to travel to the United States. Yet, here in Ireland, the Catholic Primary Schools Management Association (CPSMA) thinks it is acceptable that, as your headline has it, "Just over 1 per cent of children are refused a place over baptism barrier" (February 8th) in our national primary schools.

Of course, as was explained by Rob Sadlier in the letters page on the same day, the baptism barrier is only the tip of the iceberg. The stated aim of Catholic school managers of presenting religious principles as facts in the teaching of all subjects, through what they term the "integrated curriculum", means exposure to indoctrination against their parents' wishes of even those children who fall into the 95 per cent category where, in the words of the CPSMA chairman, "we take everyone who applies". Everyone who applies to the state school system. Once again, breath-taking arrogance from a spokesperson for the Catholic Church. A state education for all children, without reference to creed or the lack of it, is a human right, full stop. – Yours, etc,
SEAMUS McKENNA,
Windy Arbour,
Dublin 14.

Certain of the people who wished to keep the status quo in relation to religion in the schools sought to maintain that there was no intention to indoctrinate children. I could not accept that.

When I was young, we had religion classes where the book of instruction was called the Catechism of the Catholic Church. This spoke of the 'doctrine of Christ'. What does one do with doctrine, I wonder now, if not indoctrinate?

THE IRISH TIMES

24-28 TARA STREET, DUBLIN 2
Friday, October 27th, 2017
irishtimes.com

Schools and teaching religion

Sir, – Diarmuid Bolger's apologia for the policy relating to religion in Irish schools under the management of the Catholic Church (October 26th) attempts to convince that the policy does not have "indoctrination or proselytising as part of its purpose". This is at odds with the existence of the so-called integrated curriculum, where Catholic religious belief is interspersed through all subjects during the school day: policy is one thing, practical effect is something else.

Mr Bolger claims that students who do not share the religious faith of the school are allowed to read or study a text that will encourage them to "grow in their own faith or spirituality". While this might mean that the works of Richard Dawkins and Christopher Hitchens, among others, all committed atheists, will soon be made available in Irish schools, I have to admit that my expectations in this regard are not very high. – Yours, etc,
   SEAMUS McKENNA,
   Windy Arbour,
   Dublin 14.

In April of 2019 I fired off a letter that had no trigger, other than the way I was feeling at the time, to, once again, complain about the patronage system in Education.

Maybe I thought that constant repetition might have an effect. Obviously, the letters editor was of the same mind.

"Constant dripping wears the stone," as the older people used to say.

THE IRISH TIMES

24-28 TARA STREET, DUBLIN 2
Monday, April 22nd, 2019
irishtimes.com

Patronage system for education is wrong

Sir, – The patronage system for education, regardless of what organisation is given the benefit of it, is anachronistic and totally inappropriate for a modern state.

It might have been just about acceptable in the days when those in power had no regard for general education, when the ruling elites were content to have their own children, mainly their sons, educated, and then leave it at that as far as the rest of the population was concerned.

They would never have dreamed of giving the army, the police, the legal system, or any of the other functions of the state, to a patron. It is nothing short of shameful that the Irish Government of today, which is supposed to preside over the operation of a democratic republic, still holds general education in such low esteem. – Yours, etc,
SEAMUS McKENNA,
Windy Arbour,
Dublin 14.

Comparative religion studies

Whenever the subject of religion comes up in relation to schools, particularly primary schools, the question of what exactly is religious education arises. For secularists it means giving children some idea of the history and beliefs of the major world religions, with a view to engendering tolerance and understanding. For non-secularists it means concentrating on the tenets of one particular religion, with a view to establishing and strengthening the adherence of the pupils to that religion. This is nothing more or less than indoctrination, and is a million miles away from the comparative study of the tenets of different religions. This has been the basis for some extreme examples of sleight-of-hand over the years, where religious zealots have sought to confuse one with the other in order to maintain the status quo.

I felt it was important to relate that distinction to the terms of the Irish Constitution.

Religious education and faith formation

Sir, – Recent discussion of religion in State-funded schools in your letters page includes reference to the Constitution. I believe this is a mistake. The provisions of the Constitution are often ambiguous.

For example, we now differentiate between religious education, or the comparative study of different religions, and religious instruction, which is faith formation or indoctrination (John Collins, Letters, December 19th).

There can be little doubt but that the framers of the Constitution made no such distinction.

Their understanding of the subject matter of Article 42.1 is the inculcation of one particular religion's doctrine in the children of the school concerned.

The salient fact is that it is completely inappropriate for the country we have now (Derval Duggan, letters on the same day).

As with many other provisions of the Constitution that have been found wanting, such as the clauses that specify the subjugation of women, the sectarian nature of the early state, and so on, this one needs to be removed.

In the short-term I suppose we could do the old Jesuitical trick of the abuse of casuistry and represent that Éamon de Valera and those who had some influence on him at the time, such as John Charles McQuaid, did indeed see a need for the study of the characteristics of all those other religions by the children attending our primary schools, but where would that get us? – Yours, etc,
SEAMUS McKENNA,
Dublin 14.

Regular Irish Times columnist Breda O'Brien lamented, in 2021, that state schools that were under the management of the Catholic Church were beginning to look like secular schools, except for "some remaining traditions and trappings."

I suppose I could have taken that as some kind of progress in the drive for a secular school system, but I didn't. Instead, I pressed home the attack, writing that they were not Catholic schools, but Irish taxpayers' schools.

THE IRISH TIMES

24-28 TARA STREET, DUBLIN 2
Tuesday, February 9th, 2021
irishtimes.com

Catholic schools

Sir, – Breda O'Brien is concerned that, "Many Catholic schools are indistinguishable from secular schools except for some remaining traditions and trappings".

It can be argued that the great majority of the schools she is referencing cannot fairly be called Catholic schools. They are, in truth, Irish taxpayers' schools which, through an accident of history, have been placed under the management of the Catholic Church. As Irish taxpayers' schools, they should indeed be secular, with faith formation taken care of outside of the school by those parents and pastors (not teachers on State-funded salaries) who are interested in it. – Yours, etc,
SEAMUS McKENNA,
Dublin 14.

It has long been a claim of the managers of schools under Catholic management in Ireland that they are inclusive. And, indeed, the do make a good effort when it comes to welcoming the children of religions from outside of Christianity. It is almost as if they see a believer from any religion as some kind of a confederate against the common enemy, unbelief.

The onset of a greater understanding of gender diversity has been a heavy blow to Catholicism, with its absolute and unyielding condemnation of gay culture, all of which has been further complicated for them by the emergence from the shadows of people who identify as transgender.

I addressed these issues in the following letter:

Religion and sex education

Sir, – Catholic-managed primary schools, which make up over 90 per cent of State-funded primary schools, have long claimed to be inclusive. In practice, this inclusivity is selective. Children of other religions seem to find a better welcome than those of parents who want nothing to do with religion at all.

Now the Catholic Church has decided to embrace sex education, after its fashion ("Sex education and Catholic schools", Letters, April 28th, and "Religion and sex education", Letters, April 29th). However, its recent pronouncement on same-sex blessings, denounced for its "vicious language" by our former president Mary McAleese, must make it impossible for the church to offer inclusivity any longer. This is because gender diversity is a fact. It is obvious that those children who are beginning to realise that they do not conform to the Judeo-Christian, heterosexual model of gender alignment will be comprehensively rejected in schools that are operated by the Catholic Church.

The Government has a fundamental responsibility here. It must ensure that all State-funded schools are run along lines that do not discriminate, full stop. – Yours, etc,

SEAMUS McKENNA,
Dublin 14.

Advances undermined

In January of 2023 I became aware of advice that had been given to State schools under Catholic management by the Catholic Primary Schools Management Association, a lobby group that had a Public Relations professional as its Director General, which seemed to completely undermine any advances that might have been made in the past number of years in relation to creating a non-discriminatory school system. You can read the advice, and my response to it, in the following letter.

THE IRISH TIMES

24-28 TARA STREET, DUBLIN 2
Wednesday, January 4th, 2023
irishtimes.com

Schools and faith formation

Sir, –The Catholic bishops regard over 90 per cent of the primary schools in the country to be "Catholic schools" (News, January 3rd). As long as these schools are funded by taxpayers money, such an attitude is incompatible with equity, and with the Constitution. The church had always claimed that there is room in "their" schools for children from all faiths and none. Yet, in September 2016, the Catholic Primary Schools Management Association chose to issue a document to its members, entitled "Ethos in Action". This advises, among other things, the following:

"Create a school prayer space in a common area/ lobby space of the school. This should be seen by all visitors to your school who can clearly see the lived ethos of your school. Create a rota of classes/teachers and pupils to take responsibility for the school prayer space each month: This gives pupils and staff ownership of the space and ensures it changes regularly in line with the liturgical year. This school prayer space should reflect the work done by teachers in their class prayer spaces. Using prayer each day and at the beginning of all school meetings reminds of our mission as Catholic schools. This is a real and practical way of living out Ethos with the entire school community."

There are many similar guides provided by the CPSMA.

These give the lie to the oft-repeated claim that children can be opted out of faith formation, and as long as such an attitude continues, there is no hope whatsoever that public, State-funded primary schools in Ireland can ever serve the needs of the whole population.
– Yours, etc,
SEAMUS
McKENNA,
Dublin 14.

Chapter SIX

Institutional child abuse

From about 1996, when the RTE documentary "Dear daughter", directed by Louis Lentin, was broadcast, and Christine Buckley revealed the extensive and horrific abuse she had received as a child at the Goldenbridge orphanage in Dublin, there had been consistent rumblings about institutional physical and sexual abuse in Ireland. The Cloyne report was one such, and its findings were grim. Then, in 2009, The Ryan Report, officially the Report of the Commission to Inquire into Child Abuse, blew the lid off the scandal in a big way.

In the years since there have been many other reports and enquiries, all pointing to the same thing: that sexual and physical abuse of young children was almost systemic in Irish institutions, the great majority of which were under Catholic religious control and management. Of course, the problem was greatly exacerbated by the practice, directed from the very top of the church in Rome, of covering up all cases to ensure that no one outside would ever find out what was happening. Particularly insidious was the order that was given to move offending priests to other parishes and schools without telling the managers or parents in the new locations that the person in question was likely to offend again. And offend they did, in spades, and for a long time with impunity.

A celibate clergy

I thought that having a celibate clergy in charge of the education and well-being of children was a bad idea, and I wrote accordingly to the editor of The Irish Times, as follows:

THE IRISH TIMES

Letters

Tue Dec 30 2008 - 00:00

Church, State and child abuse

Madam, – The juxtaposition of the banking crisis and the Cloyne report in your Letters page is apt. The Irish public, and parents in particular, should take a leaf from the stockbrokers who want nothing to do with Anglo Irish Bank, according to your business and finance correspondents. This is called facing reality.

It is time the nation faced the reality of how deplorably disastrous it was always going to be to have the vast majority of our primary education system under the management of a celibate clergy, with its tendency to attract some members whose attitude to children is unwholesome and with all the rest, by definition, cut off from the balancing influence of female companionship and the essential edifying experience for educators that can only be gained by at least the possibility of having offspring of their own. – Yours, etc,

SEAMUS McKENNA,
Farrenboley Park,
Windy Arbour,
Dublin 14.

This was responded to by a Father James Good, who wrote:

THE IRISH TIMES

24-28 TARA STREET, DUBLIN 2
WEDNESDAY, JANUARY 14TH, 2009
www.irishtimes.com

Catholic Church and celibacy

Madam, – Seamus McKenna (December 30th) tells us that "the essential edifying experience for educators... can only be gained by at least the possibility of having offspring of their own".

Mr McKenna does not seem to have adverted to the interesting consequences of his theory. Among other things, it would involve the instant dismissal from their posts of all unmarried post-menopausal teachers, as well as compulsory fertility tests for all trainee teachers. Agreed?

He also believes that celibate clergy are "by definition, cut off from the balancing influence of female companionship". I must confess that (I am now in my middle 80s) I never felt cut off from this delightful source of balancing influence – whenever I needed "balance".

Mr McKenna does not seem to have learned from history that if it were not for the influence of the brothers and sisters (and their clerical managers) we Irish might be still picking morsels of food from municipal dumps instead of being the well-educated people that we are. – Yours, etc,

Fr JAMES GOOD,
Douglas,
Cork.

I did not want to have a prolonged correspondence involving the examples given by Fr. Good to back up his argument, and in any event I did not believe the Letters Editor would have countenanced such a debate. I still held to the view that compulsory celibacy was a bad thing for people who were put in charge of young people.

I was, also, particularly concerned about the belief, held by a great many proponents of denominational education, that the Catholic Church had been responsible, all on its own, for the education system in the county. As can be seen from the section above on education in Ireland, the overriding concern of the Catholic hierarchy at all times was that it should *control* education, regardless of who paid for it.

THE IRISH TIMES

Letters

Tuesday, January 20, 2009

Catholic Church and celibacy

Madam, – Having a whole class of people take a lifetime vow that they will never have a conjugal relationship is a grave interference with nature. One interferes with nature at one's peril.

Such a relationship involves compromise, negotiation and sharing on a permanent, minute-by-minute basis. On the other side of the ledger comes companionship, support, being forced more often than one might like to face reality about oneself – and last, but by no means least, sexual fulfilment. If children do come they bring a component that is at once sublime and extremely challenging.

Of course there will be individuals who will not conform to the standard model.

They demonstrate essential personal freedom of choice and, sometimes, provide the elements of welcome diversity that nature itself has evolved.

The crucial factor is that they have not predisposed themselves to never knowing a sexual relationship. Even Fr James Good's unmarried post-menopausal teacher (January 14th) will not necessarily have done that unless, of course, she is a member of a religious order.

In nature the sex drive is an extremely potent force. On occasions it overpowers everything else. Some of the perpetrators of sexual abuse are otherwise not bad people. Many of them have gone tragically wrong, even when married and with children. Therefore, at the best of times, dealing with sex is fraught.

No judgment in the matter of celibacy as a group policy can be made on the basis of individual cases or experiences. But when thousands of people involved with the welfare of children turn their communal face against the corrective of a relationship, they are not giving themselves as a body, or the young people who come into their charge, a chance.

The canard that Ireland would have no education were it not for religious orders needs also to be disposed of.

In our country the Hierarchy appropriated education (and health) in order to gain control and pursue their own agenda, which was not primarily even the kind of education best suited to an industrialised nation.

Continued…

...continued.

There is no evidence at all to suggest that, in the absence of religious involvement, a proper, government-managed educational system would not have been set up. After all, we have well established judicial, taxation, local authority, military and police systems, to name but some, all without any religious participation in their creation. – Yours, etc,

SEAMUS McKENNA,
**Farrenboley Park,
Windy Arbour,
Dublin 14.**

Government reports on abuse in state institutions

The reverberations of the Ryan and other similar reports provided much fodder for people, like me, who wrote to the editor of The Irish Times regularly. Patsy McGarry, long time religious correspondent of the paper, also had much to say on the topic. I responded to a piece he had in the Opinion section in May 2009. Note that this anticipated the controversy that would take place later on the subject of human reproduction, and such things as stem cell research.

THE IRISH TIMES

Letters Mon May 25 2009

Response to Ryan report on child abuse in State institutions

Madam, – "It takes an extraordinary perversity of nature to thwart the instinctive drive to nurture and care for the young" (Patsy McGarry, Analysis, May 21st). Very true, but religion will do it. From a philosophy that holds that the corporal body is of no account and must be mortified, to superstitions about left-handedness, stammering or any other form of diversity being deviant and the work of the devil, there was more than enough to enable normal human decency to be well and truly buried, especially in an institutional setting.

Nobel Prize winner Steven Weinberg said it best: "With or without it [religion] you would have good people doing good things and evil people doing evil things. But for good people to do evil things, that takes religion".

There is a clear line of descent from the archaic beliefs that allowed the abuse to happen so comprehensively to the thinking today that underpins Ireland's deplorable approach to abortion and stem cell research legislation. It is high time we properly separated church and state. – Yours, etc,

SEAMUS McKENNA,
Farrenboley Park,
Windy Arbour
Dublin 14

Then Fintan O'Toole weighed in with his opinion: In a piece entitled "Lessons in the power of the church", in June of 2009 he dealt comprehensively with the issue that has been exercising us here. In the course of the article he wrote:

> "The great myth that hangs over so much discussion of the Catholic Church's domination of the education and health systems is that the church stepped in to offer services that the State refused to provide. Had it not been for the church, the story goes, the plain people of Ireland would have been left without schools or medical services.
>
> While there is some truth to this belief in relation to the conditions of the early 19th century, it is largely wrong. Indeed, the opposite is nearer the truth – the church consistently undermined State services, fought to limit their expansion and consistently put the maintenance of its own power ahead of the interests of vulnerable people."

At the end of the article he says this:

> "The reality is that Ireland ended up with its anomalous system of church control in education and health, not by default, but by design. The design was the church's determination that these services be delivered, not as the universal right of citizens, but as gifts of its own benevolence.
>
> This has left us with a system in which, for example, the religious orders named in the Ryan report for inflicting and covering up systemic child abuse still control around 1,000 primary schools. The church not only insists on retaining this power, but is demanding that in any new system that takes account of the increasing diversity of Irish society, the church would still be joint patron of schools. Power built up over 150 years will not be easily ceded, but until it is, neither the church nor the State will be free to face up to its responsibilities."

The entire article is available on the Irish Times website. You might be subject to a paywall (journalists do need to be paid, and newspapers do need to keep the light on, after all) but in any event it can be accessed here:

https://www.irishtimes.com/news/lessons-in-the-power-of-the-church-1.778683

THE IRISH TIMES

Letters   Wed Jun 10 2009

Response to Ryan report on child abuse in State institutions

Madam, – Not for the first time we owe a debt of gratitude to Fintan O'Toole for a superbly researched article that we might venture to hope will prove to be pivotal. ("Lessons in the power of the church", Weekend Review, June 6th).

I believe this is the articulation, on the back of the Ryan commission report revelations, that has the potential to finally bring to an end the bizarre domination of the management of our primary school system by one particular religious grouping.

This article, Madam, should be made into a pamphlet and then distributed to every home in the country. – Yours, etc,

SEAMUS McKENNA,
Farrenboley Park,
Windy Arbour
Dublin 14

Taoiseach Enda Kenny excoriates the Catholic Church

The church went into a very powerful damage limitation mode when the extent of the scandal of institutional child abuse became clear. It took out insurance to protect itself against claims, and hired expensive legal and Public Relations expertise to face the media once it found that it was no longer possible to keep secret the facts of what had been taking place.

There was a reaction to that too. On July 20th, 2011, the then Taoiseach, Enda Kenny, made a speech to the Dail. This was his and the government's reaction to the Cloyne report. Its opening stanzas were as follows:

> "The revelations of the Cloyne report have brought the Government, Irish Catholics and the Vatican to an unprecedented juncture.
> It's fair to say that after the Ryan and Murphy Reports Ireland is, perhaps, unshockable when it comes to the abuse of children.
> But Cloyne has proved to be of a different order.
> Because for the first time in Ireland, a report into child sexual-abuse exposes an attempt by the Holy See to frustrate an Inquiry in a sovereign, democratic republic…as little as three years ago, not three decades ago.
> And in doing so, the Cloyne Report excavates the dysfunction, disconnection, elitism....the narcissism ....that dominate the culture of the Vatican to this day.
> The rape and torture of children were downplayed or 'managed' to uphold instead, the primacy of the institution, its power, standing and 'reputation'.
> Far from listening to evidence of humiliation and betrayal with St Benedict's "ear of the heart"......the Vatican's reaction was to parse and analyse it with the gimlet eye of a canon lawyer.
> This calculated, withering position being the polar opposite of

the radicalism, humility and compassion upon which the Roman Church was founded.

The radicalism, humility and compassion which are the very essence of its foundation and purpose.

The behaviour being a case of Roma locuta est: causa finita est. [*Rome has spoken; the case is closed. My translation*, SMcK]

Except in this instance, nothing could be further from the truth.

Victims

Cloyne's revelations are heart-breaking. It describes how many victims continued to live in the small towns and parishes in which they were reared and in which they were abused... Their abuser often still in the area and still held in high regard by their families and the community. The abusers continued to officiate at family weddings and funerals... In one case, the abuser even officiated at the victim's own wedding...

There is little I or anyone else in this House can say to comfort that victim or others, however much we want to. But we can and do recognise the bravery of all of the victims who told their stories to the Commission.

While it will take a long time for Cloyne to recover from the horrors uncovered, it could take the victims and their families a lifetime to pick up the pieces of their shattered existence."

The speech went on for quite a bit more, and you can read the whole of it here: https://www.irishtimes.com/news/taoiseach-s-speech-on-cloyne-motion-1.880466 This was my response:

THE IRISH TIMES

Letters

Taoiseach's speech and Cloyne

Tue Jul 26 2011

Sir, – The Taoiseach was right when he said: "Far from listening to evidence of humiliation and betrayal with St Benedict's 'ear of the heart' ... the Vatican's reaction was to parse and analyse it with the gimlet eye of a canon lawyer". Vincent Twomey's article (Opinion Analysis, July 25th) merely carries on this long-standing but deplorable tradition. – Yours, etc,

SEAMUS McKENNA,
Farrenboley Park,
Windy Arbour, Dublin 14

Of course the matter did not end there. There was more correspondence in the paper and, on Sept 8th 2011, I was able to answer the charge, by some, that ordinary people in Ireland at the time were also culpable for what went on.

THE IRISH TIMES

Letters

Vatican response to Cloyne report

Thu Sept 08 2011

Sir, – Many commentators claim the abuse of children and vulnerable adults in the past was as much the responsibility of the State as it was of the churches that managed the various institutions. Thus Dermot Keogh (Opinion, September 6th) writes: "There were many so-called bystanders when crimes were committed against the weakest and most vulnerable".

It's not that simple. Because the professions and the wide section of society mentioned by Dr Keogh, including, most notably, the political establishment and the civil service, were in thrall to the Catholic hierarchy, to a level that seems incredible today, there was really no distinction to be made between church and State. There were, therefore, very few bystanders, and none with any power.

Now that we seem to have an appreciation for democracy and the rights of the individual, we should reasonably expect a long overdue separation of church as State. In particular, we need to reclaim our national schools so that children can, at the level of State involvement in their education, learn how to think, rather than what to think, and thereby avoid the possibility of them being subjected to the disastrous indoctrination that was the lot of their recent forebears. – Yours, etc,

SEAMUS McKENNA,
Farrenboley Park,
Windy Arbour,
Dublin 14.

Almost exactly eight years later I was motivated to repeat the same point:

THE IRISH TIMES

24-28 TARA STREET, DUBLIN 2
Thursday, September 6th, 2018
irishtimes.com

Church and State in 20th-century Ireland

Sir, – Dr Martin Hanrahan (September 3rd) is at pains to point out that Irish society generally had a responsibility for the terrible things that were done to women, and to children and other vulnerable people, in the past, and not just those who were within the Catholic Church.

Anyone who lived at the time would know that in the Ireland of the middle decades of the last century, the whole country, from the most senior politician down, was in thrall to the Catholic Church.

Members of the Civil Service and of those institutions that had power were very often also members of church organisations, some of them secret organisations. In their day jobs they complemented perfectly all that the church was doing, and did their utmost to maintain church dominance. The general public accepted without question that if a priest, let alone a bishop, made a pronouncement, it was the last word that could ever be spoken on the subject.

Those few individuals who had the temerity to speak out or to try to do something concrete to improve matters, such as Dr Noël Browne, minister for health from 1948 to 1951, were very effectively silenced by their superiors, who were well able to anticipate what the hierarchy would want to see happening.

The simple fact of the matter is that in every practical sense, there was no "Irish society generally" that could be differentiated from the Catholic Church. And that was the problem. –
Yours, etc,
SEAMUS McKENNA,
Windy Arbour,
Dublin 14.

Sometimes I got a little cross with the attitudes of some of my opponents on the letters page. Rightly or wrongly, I occasionally formed the impression that they were being more than a little bit obtuse. I suppose all who indulge in argument feel like this from time to time.

A letter writer from Co. Waterford wrote:

THE IRISH TIMES

13 D'OLIER STREET, DUBLIN 2
SATURDAY, SEPTEMBER 17TH 2011

Letters

Respecting matters of faith

Sat Sept 17 2011 - 01:00

Sir, – If a man walked out on his wife and family, most readers of *The Irish Times* would, no doubt, suspend judgment, respecting the essentially private nature of his decision. If the same man, however, then proceeded to publicly criticise his wife, *ad nauseam, ad infinitum*, and insisted on telling all and sundry how badly she handled the raising of their children, these same readers would not be too impressed. To use an old-fashioned word, such behaviour would be regarded as caddish.

Surely the same standards should apply to lapsed Catholics, of which your newspaper seems to have more than its share, both columnists and readers? Your reasons for deserting us are your own business, and those of us who still practise do not stand in judgment on you; so please, please, stop moaning about us and telling us how we might do things better. – Yours, etc,

JIM STACK,
Moneygorm South,
Lismore, Co Waterford.

This was my response:

THE IRISH TIMES

Letters

Respecting matters of faith

Tue Sept 20 2011

Sir, – If a man walked out on his wife and did not want to appear a cad he would, indeed, pace Jim Stack (September 17th), not criticise her previous behaviour. However, if the same wife insisted on continuing to meddle in the man's life he would be well justified in calling for her to desist.

As soon as the Catholic Church hands back the running of our national schools so that children from families of all faiths and none can receive a State-funded education without discriminatory entry requirements, in an environment that is not shot through with the propaganda and artefacts of that religion; as soon as the church guarantees that it will not attempt to influence the laws and Constitution of this country so that its precepts effectively stand between a doctor and his or her patient; as soon as we have a situation where the Catholic Church does not continuously impinge on my life unless I wish it to, then Mr Stack and each and every one of his co-religionists can proceed without a word from me. I will in fact, to paraphrase Voltaire, defend, to the death, his and their right to do so.

– Yours, etc,

SEAMUS McKENNA, Farrenboley Park, Windy Arbour, Dublin 14.

Chapter SEVEN

Abortion in Ireland

In 1983 an amendment, which guaranteed the equal right to life of the unborn child with that of its mother, was included in the Irish Constitution. This had the effect of outlawing abortion in any and all circumstances. Such is the default position of the Catholic Church, and that institution was the most important driver of the decision by the people to carry the referendum that authorised the amendment.

There were many alarums and excursions in the following years as a result of this, the eighth amendment to the Constitution. The most important of these was the establishment of a right of someone who was pregnant to travel to another jurisdiction to have a termination, but not before an unfortunate girl of fifteen, who had become pregnant as a result of rape, was prevented from travelling, with her parents, when it became known that the purpose of her trip was to have an abortion. The public outcry over this resulted in the establishment of an absolute right to travel, even if the purpose of the trip was to terminate a pregnancy. This was the notorious X case.

In 2018 the eighth amendment was repealed. This outcome did not come easily. There were many years of campaigning, arguing, serious impact on the health of women, and even the death of at least one, because of the ban on abortion. In the meantime, we had to have a debate on frozen embryos.

For many couples, the only route to pregnancy is via In Vitro Fertilisation, or IVF. The Catholic Church is opposed to this procedure. One of its abiding principles has it that every human has an immortal soul, and this soul comes into being at the time of conception, i.e., when a human egg is fertilised by a human spermatozoon (a single mobile sperm cell). All souls must be "saved", or cleaned of Original Sin, which happens in baptism. A fertilised egg, or embryo, cannot be baptised, so the Catholic Church is against IVF. It continues to hold this view in the face of the fact that so many infertile couples, a great many of whom are adherents to Catholicism, go ahead anyway and use the procedure.

Frozen embryos

In 2006 the Eight Amendment was still in force, which might have given comfort to Catholics who wanted IVF to be outlawed under the principle of the equal right to life of the unborn. However, in 2001 a Supreme Court judgement found that the equal right to life only applied after the implantation of the embryo in the uterus. It would seem that the courts took the view that cryogenically frozen fertilised eggs were not living beings, as the church held, but merely organisms that had the potential to become human.

I wrote the two letters below to the Irish Times at that stage. Looking back, they would have represented early shots in the campaign to repeal the Eighth.

THE IRISH TIMES
24-28 Tara Street, Dublin 2
DECEMBER 7TH 2006

Ruling on frozen embryos

Madam, – D. Vincent Twomey's letter of December 4th in response to Tom Moore's of November 23rd is, at once, objectionable and self-contradictory. Objectionable because he uses the reprehensible behaviour of the Nazis to, in the most irrational manner, attempt to denigrate science and self-contradictory because he writes of the "absolute claims" of science while, in the same letter, acknowledging that science is constantly correcting its claims. The latter is the right understanding. It is called the scientific method and it is what gives science its power and its beauty. A hypothesis is put forward, is tested and, if found wanting, is rejected in favour of a better theory.

No matter how much emotional capital has been invested in an idea, if it fails to stand up to rigorous testing, the scientist abandons it and moves on.

The letter involves seriously muddled thinking. How can the writer infer a tendency to descend into inhuman experimentation from Tom Moore's comments, which, it seems to me, are far more likely to lead to vegetarianism and a ban on vivisection than anything else? Vincent Twomey writes of the intuitions of common sense. Common sense tells me that men cannot come back from the dead (as opposed from recovering from a comatose state). Common sense tells me that if I kill infidels and take my own life in the process, there will not be 72 virgins waiting for me in heaven.

Common sense tells me that people cannot walk on water in depth in its liquid state and, if they are perceived to have turned water into wine, the explanation is far more likely to involve the techniques of conjuring and illusion (or simple misunderstanding on the part of reporters of the incident) than that the chemical composition of the liquid has spontaneously changed to create what would normally require the addition of crushed grapes and weeks of fermentation.

Lastly, it is way beyond time for individuals like Vincent Twomey to get over the conceit that religion is a necessary precondition, or some kind of a guarantee, of morality. A cursory glance at even recent history will reveal that this is not the case. – Yours, etc,
SEAMUS McKENNA,
Dundrum,
Dublin 14.

THE IRISH TIMES
24-28 Tara Street, Dublin 2

27th December 2006

Church and State

Madam, – A lot of the criticism in your letters pages regarding the recent ruling on frozen embryos Mr Justice McGovern has come from Roman Catholic priests. This included an attack on science by the professor of moral theology in Maynooth, to which you were recently good enough to publish my response.

It is important, at this stage, to remind ourselves about the situation that existed when the Catholic Church had the ability to influence legislation in this State. We had laws against divorce and contraception, not to mention censorship laws which were applied in an outrageous fashion. If they could have been policed, I have little doubt we would have had laws against masturbation and extra-marital sex. The effect the church had on people's minds certainly engendered great feelings of guilt in relation to those activities.

We still have an absolute ban on abortion, though the people have overwhelmingly stopped short of preventing travel to obtain one and we seem to have no difficulty in publicising abortion services abroad. This must mean that a majority believes that abortion is justified in certain circumstances.

Issues such as the treatment of frozen embryos and, indeed, abortion, cannot be seen in the simplistic, ban-everything terms that existed in the past. They have to be subject to sensible decision-making based on compassionate ethics, as opposed to the blind application of a "revealed" moral code.

The good news is that, as in the case of the reproductive and sexual matters referred to above, Irish people have shown themselves to be capable of this.

On the question of abortion, the slogan adopted by the Clintons, Hillary and Bill, to the effect that it should be "safe, legal and rare" seems to me to be a good place to make a start. – Yours, etc,
SEAMUS McKENNA,
Farrenboley Park,
Windy Arbour,
Dublin 14.

Some years later, in 2017, the treatment of embryos was still exercising correspondents. Another prolific contributor to the letters page, the Rev. Patrick J. Burke, made it clear that he regarded the start of human life as being at conception. I couldn't resist the urge to respond.

THE IRISH TIMES
24-28 TARA STREET, DUBLIN 2
Tuesday, August 8th, 2017
irishtimes.com

Genetic editing of human embryos

Sir, – Human gene editing might well be unethical, but I, for one, will not be applying to the religious for guidance on the matter. The Rev Patrick J Burke (August 5th) believes that human life begins at the moment of conception. I believe that what exists immediately after conception, and until the foetus becomes viable, is something that has the potential to become a person, in exactly the same way that a spermatozoon has the potential to become a person.

To be consistent, the Revd Burke and his religious colleagues should be calling for an outright ban on the use of condoms and other, similar, forms of contraception. But wait, the Catholic Church, at least, does have such a ban. It is just that most, if not all, of its adherents totally ignore it, and it has never managed to have it written into the Constitution of the State. – Yours, etc,
SEAMUS McKENNA,
Windy Arbour, Dublin 14.

The debate on frozen embryos did indeed turn out to be among the first shots fired in what would become the campaign to repeal the Eighth Amendment, which was the legal basis for the outlawing of abortion in any and all circumstances.

The X case (see introduction, above) was an important motivator for the people who supported this movement. In February of 2012 I wrote in response to a letter that had been published in defence of the ban on abortion. The writer argued that if the majority in a state wanted something, then it should become the law. I believed then, and believe now, that minorities have rights.

THE IRISH TIMES

Letters

Recalling the X case

Wed Feb 08 2012

Sir, – From the comments in her letter (February 7th), Katie Robinson of Youth Defence seems to be one of those people who sees democracy only in terms of the will and dominance of the majority.

But majorities can be just as tyrannical as the worst dictator. That is why the free world operates a system of constitutional democracy, which has other elements in the mix, such as parliamentary representation and a constitution that guarantees the rights, not only of minorities, but of the individual.

By failing to legislate for abortion, our politicians have manifestly failed to uphold this principle, not least for the many thousands of women who have been and are obliged to travel abroad, year after year after year, in order to have their terminations. –

Yours, etc,

SEAMUS McKENNA,
Farrenboley Park,
Windy Arbour, Dublin 14.

I made the same point in regard to school patronage at the end of 2012.

THE IRISH TIMES

24-28 TARA STREET, DUBLIN 2
Thursday, December 20th, 2012

Changing school patronage

Sir, – AM Kehoe (December 19th) believes, like too many, that democracy allows for tyrannical behaviour by a majority. What we are supposed to have here in Ireland is a constitutional democracy, which holds that minorities have certain inalienable rights.

Foremost among these is the right to an education, free from religious indoctrination if that is what is required.

To regard it as legitimate that any percentage of a region's parents should be obliged to have their children educated in State-funded schools in an atmosphere of ubiquitous religious symbolism – having to go somewhere apart when religious ceremony and direct instruction takes place and with the incorporation of religious principles in all subjects taught throughout the school day – when they do not want this, is to support a straightforward negation of their civil rights.

The solution is clear: religious instruction should be given in the home or in the appropriate place of worship. Schools and especially State schools, which are funded by all taxpayers, should be places where children are taught how to think, not what to think. – Yours, etc,
SEAMUS McKENNA,
Farrenboley Park,
Windy Arbour, Dublin 14.

I was able to indulge myself as an amateur historian in the letters pages too. As the debate on abortion gathered pace I submitted the following offering, which made the connection between the breaking of the link with Rome during the time of Henry VIII, the subsequent Reformation, and the activities of some of those who combined the desire to go back to Rome and, at the same time, to get out from under the colonial domination of Great Britain.

THE IRISH TIMES

Letters

The abortion debate

Thu May 09 2013 - 06:00

Sir, – Dr Jacky Jones is correct (Health + Family, May 7th). But while the misogyny is present, it is not at all a natural part of the Irish psyche. It is a hangover from the bizarre domination of the majority of the population by Catholicism that has existed since the Reformation, after which Irish independence aspirations were inextricably linked to support for that religion. This link was strongly reinforced during the ascendancy, such as it was, of Hugh O'Neill, Earl of Tyrone, and later through his relatively powerful kinsman, Eoin Roe O'Neill, during the time of the Catholic Confederation of Kilkenny. It was very strong just before and certainly right after actual Independence.

There has to be some correlation between the fact that the Reformation passed nationalist Ireland by and the enmity that existed between England and the Catholic powers of late medieval Europe in Spain, France and the Vatican. Irish nationalists, it would seem, saw England's difficulties as Ireland's opportunities and acted accordingly, nailing their colours to the Catholic mast in the process.

Whatever the history, we are now playing the endgame in the effort to have the irrational belief in the immortal soul and Catholicism's despising of women separated, once and for all, from the business of running the State in the interests of all its citizens.

The trend, at least, is in the right direction. – Yours, etc,

SEAMUS McKENNA,
Farrenboley Park,
Windy Arbour, Dublin 14.

The campaign to repeal the Eight Amendment

My belief was that we needed a regulated abortion regime in Ireland, and that those who opposed abortion in any and all circumstances, because they followed Catholic Church teaching on the matter, were making it impossible for regulation to take place. They were polarising the debate, and I was able to make this point in September of 2015.

THE IRISH TIMES

24-28 TARA STREET, DUBLIN 2
Friday, September 18th, 2015
irishtimes.com

The Eighth Amendment

Sir, – I believe that Maria Mhic Mheanmain (September 16th) is correct when she says that people are deeply uncomfortable with abortion (and they are not just in Ireland). I know I am. But I also accept that there are cases where it can be warranted.

Those who would ban abortion in all cases, under any and all circumstances, are polarising the debate.

Many of the people who deny that there are any occasions when an abortion might take place have the existence of the immortal soul as their basis for so doing.

This is their right under freedom of religion but they have no right to use something that is an impossible concept for so many to accept in order to have the ensuing beliefs written into the law of the land, and to create a situation where there is no room for those who would argue for a responsible but highly restrictive abortion regime in this country. – Yours, etc,
SEAMUS McKENNA,
Windy Arbour,
Dublin 14.

We all argued, and still do, about the question of when human life begins. This is fundamental for the issue of whether abortion should be allowed at all, even in a well-regulated way.

THE IRISH TIMES

24-28 TARA STREET, DUBLIN 2
Friday, October 6th, 2017
irishtimes.com

The Eighth Amendment

Sir, – Brendan O'Regan's letter (October 5th) makes clear the distinction between those who support his standpoint and those who would allow for abortion under certain circumstances.

Mr O'Regan's position is that of the Christian philosophical tradition, which holds that the immortal soul, and therefore life, comes into being at the moment of conception. Many other decent, compassionate people regard the criteria for life to be the desirability of the pregnancy sustaining it until such time as viability and/or sentience are present. No baby, no unborn child, exists until then.

The intervening period provides an opportunity for modern scientific medical systems to ascertain that the resulting child will have a quality of life after birth. Otherwise an abortion should be allowed. This is the case in other civilised jurisdictions.

As with all matters involving the dogmatic certitude of religion, these positions are absolutely irreconcilable.

The only possible solution here is that religious adherents should be free to follow their beliefs themselves, but should not have the ability to force others, through the application of the law, to be bound by principles to which they do not themselves subscribe. – Yours, etc,
SEAMUS McKENNA,
Windy Arbour,
Dublin 14.

No sooner had we arrived at a situation where women with crisis pregnancies could consider terminations in Ireland, than the people who wanted an absolute ban decided to picket those clinics that offered the service. If they had left it that there would have been no problems, but they did not. They started to follow the example of the far-right evangelists in the United States, who harass and abuse, in the most violent manner, the unfortunate women who find themselves in a position where they must make their way to such facilities.

The abuse got so bad that the government began to consider the possibility of creating safe zones around the clinics, and they also appealed for privacy for the women who needed to visit them. Fr. Gregory O'Brien, a Parish Priest, made it very clear that he was not in favour, in the slightest, of providing such privacy.

I wrote to challenge him.

THE IRISH TIMES

24-28 TARA STREET, DUBLIN 2
Thursday, February 21st, 2019
irishtimes.com

Abortion and privacy

Sir, – The comments of Fr Gregory O'Brien PP, (February 20th) are utterly chilling in their absolutism and in their willingness to target a single, very probably vulnerable individual to receive punitive treatment for the perceived wrongdoings of a whole society, where many thousands of others have been accessing the same procedure every year, but were obliged to travel abroad to do so.

Those of Fr Gregory's mindset are quite happy to ignore the fact that in any single case where a termination of pregnancy is desired the reasons for it will be both complex and, by the criteria of ordinary people who are not as absolutist as a dedicated follower of the Roman Catholic tradition or, in the case of other countries, the evangelical Christian hard right wing, well justified. – Yours, etc,
SEAMUS MCKENNA,
Dublin 14.

This was followed up by a letter on August 5th 2022, which built on the same argument.

THE IRISH TIMES

24-28 TARA STREET, DUBLIN 2
Friday, August 5th, 2022
irishtimes.com

Protection from intimidation

Sir, – Your correspondent, Trevor Troy (Letters, August 4th), obviously cannot see the difference between the right to express an opinion and the right for a vulnerable individual to be protected from intimidation, when he argues against safe access zones around abortion facilities.

There are many instances where rights that are generally protected in regard to the population at large are suspended in individual cases: we do not allow family law hearing to be made public, even though it is a basic principle of democracy that justice must not only be done but must be seen to be done; individuals can apply for protection against being accosted by such as paparazzi, and so on.

A woman in need of a termination, who has already been subjected to quite onerous qualifying criteria under the law, is entitled to be protected from those who would like to make her situation worse. – Yours, etc,

SEAMUS McKENNA,
Dublin 14.

Chapter EIGHT

Sinn Féin

The murder of Terence McKeever

After Marilyn and I got married I bought a site near the village of Convoy, in Co. Donegal, and built a house on it. Then our son Shane arrived, in 1986, to be followed by his sister Kate a little over a year later.

The so called "Troubles" in the North of Ireland were rumbling on during those years. My work as a Technical Officer with the IDA continued. I was also making friends. One of them was Terence McKeever, an electrical contractor from Co. Armagh, whose family also had an electrical appliance shop in Ballyshannon in south Donegal. Terence's company carried out electrical contracting on IDA factories. I had just completed our house, which needed a TV set. I acquired one from Terence and, yes, I probably got "mate's rates" on that particular purchase.

One day in the middle of June of 1986 I was just pulling up outside the house on my way home from work when I heard an item in the news in Irish on the car radio. My Irish was never great, but I realised that this concerned a Terence McKeever, and that something terrible had happened to him.

My worst fears were realised. On the TV news that night, on the very television set I had received from Terence, I was able to see the obscene image of his body, with a gunshot wound behind his ear, lying dead in a roadside ditch just across the border with the Republic, in South Armagh. He had been abducted by the IRA and murdered. His "crime" was that his company carried out electrical work for the Royal Ulster Constabulary (RUC).

The people who killed him were members of the Provisional Irish Republican Army (PIRA), a vicious physical-force republican outfit, of which the political wing, and main apologist, was and is Sinn Féin. An ordinary guy, who was just going about his business, had been murdered in cold blood.

There were other horrific things done by the people who had decided that they would embrace car bombs, shootings, knee-capping, bank robberies, and kidnapping in pursuit of their aims. These were things we could not ignore, no matter how much we wanted to just get on with living our lives.

In August of 1998 Marilyn and I drove back home to Donegal after a visit to Dublin. That meant crossing the border into Northern Ireland at Aughnacloy in Co. Tyrone, and travelling through the North as far as Strabane, after which we would find ourselves in Donegal, and the Republic, once again. The Tyrone County town is Omagh. In previous years one would have to drive through it, but the authorities had recently built a ring road around it. Naturally, we took that.

As we were proceeding on our way westwards, after leaving Omagh, first one, and then many more, ambulances passed us, going in the opposite direction.

"It looks like there was a very bad accident," one of us said to the other.

"I hope that's all it was."

We learned, in due course, that the centre of Omagh had just been devastated by a bomb. Ordinary people going about their business on a busy shopping afternoon (the bomb exploded on a Saturday, at 3:10 in the afternoon) had been killed or had suffered horrific injuries. In all 31 men, women and children died, and hundreds were injured. Those injured who lived, and the bereaved, had their lives changed in the most terrible manner. The entire population of the area was traumatised.

Although it later became involved in the Peace Process, which led to the Good Friday Agreement, Sinn Féin was tied inextricably to the Provisional IRA, who carried out the awful Remembrance Day bombing in Enniskillen. The activities of Martin McGuinness, Gerry Adams, and others, who were avowed members of Sinn Féin, spawned the so-called dissident republican lunatics of the later years; the Real IRA, the Continuity IRA, the New IRA, the whatever-you're-having yourself IRA. Thus McGuinnes and Adams, at the very least, helped to train the people who carried out the Omagh bombing in 1998.

In 2021 I was able to have the following letter published in the Irish Times:

THE IRISH TIMES

24-28 TARA STREET, DUBLIN 2
Wednesday, September 1st, 2021
irishtimes.com

'Moral test' for Sinn Féin

Sir, – Micheál Mac Donncha (Letters, August 31st) wants to characterise the IRA's 30-year campaign of mass killings as a conflict. That word implies that the other side had the capacity to fight back, or at least to defend itself.

This idea is made a nonsense of when one considers the ordinary men, women and children who were simply going about their normal business when Remembrance Day in Enniskillen was bombed; when the centre of Omagh was obliterated; or when civilian contractors were executed and their bodies dumped on the Border because they had the temerity to offer their services to entities that the IRA regarded as "legitimate targets".

Playing with words now will not absolve the IRA, or its apologists, of responsibility for what Fintan O'Toole has rightly called the disaster that Sinn Féin helped inflict on the Irish people.

– Yours, etc,
SEAMUS McKENNA
Windy Arbour,
Dublin 14.

Election success

Sinn Féin has had success in elections in the South, after it belatedly embraced the democratic process. It has had very good success in the North. I'm afraid I find myself unable to contribute in any way to those accomplishments.

In 2022 I got the opportunity to make my feelings known about this organisation as a political entity.

THE IRISH TIMES

24-28 TARA STREET, DUBLIN 2
Thursday, September 8th, 2022
irishtimes.com

Sinn Féin and Generation Z

Sir, – Gemma Haverty has ticked all the boxes that Sinn Féin has ostentatiously presented to the electorate in its attempts to get into power ("Sinn Féin is speaking the language of my generation, but can it deliver?, Opinion & Analysis, September 7th).

But there are other issues in its profile that it has not been so keen to highlight. It has been unable to formulate a coherent policy on the great existential subject of our time, emissions reduction, and it seems the reason for this is that it cannot decide which segment of the electorate it wants to impress the most, rural or urban. Its record in various referendums shows it is, at best, ambivalent about Ireland's role in the European Union, our membership of which is the most important political development for Ireland in any generation, including Gen Z.

It cannot be denied by anyone that Sinn Féin glorifies violence. Even as it depends on the desire of younger voters to live in the present, in order to gloss over what they were responsible for in the receding past, senior figures like Michelle O'Neill can still, right now, make remarks to the effect that the IRA had no alternative to the sickening acts of violence it perpetrated. A current frontbench member was able to shout IRA slogans in the euphoria of Sinn Féin's relative success in the last general election.

We need to take the totality of what Sinn Féin stands for into account. – Yours, etc,
SEAMUS McKENNA,
Dublin 14.

Gerry Adams and the N-word

However, in 2016 I found myself standing up for Gerry Adams, erstwhile leader of Sinn Féin. He had, apparently, just watched a screening of the Quenten Tarantino film, Django Unchained. This motivated him to make a connection between African Americans in antebellum America and Catholic Nationalists in Northern Ireland during the Stormont regime. He went on what was then Twitter, and is now known as X.

I had seen that movie myself, and enjoyed it. I was particularly taken by the fact the Tarantino was able to put words into the mouth of Samuel L. Jackson, himself black, which broke a long-standing taboo. I could understand where Adams was coming from, and I also accepted that his apology was sincere. But his use of the N-word at the time caused a furore.

Watching Django Unchained- A Ballymurphy Nigger!

The tweet from the Gerry Adams twitter account on Sunday night which was later deleted.

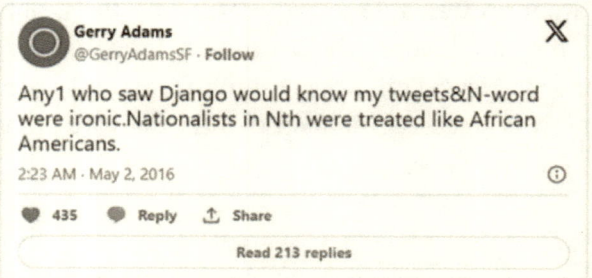

THE IRISH TIMES

24-28 TARA STREET, DUBLIN 2
Wednesday, May 4th, 2016
irishtimes.com

Gerry Adams and 'N' word tweet

Sir, – While I have never been a supporter of Sinn Féin leader Gerry Adams, and while I do not think it likely I will be voting for his party any time soon, I am struck by the rush to judgement of some commentators over his use of a term for black people which he was motivated to employ as a result of watching a Quentin Tarantino movie.

Anyone with any experience of the cinema in recent years will realise that the above named director and screenwriter, particularly through the words placed in the dialogue of one of his most used actors, Samuel L Jackson, has effectively made the use of that term acceptable again. Language is a living thing.

If it is okay for Tarantino and Jackson, I do not see why it cannot be good enough for Adams.
– Yours, etc,
SEAMUS McKENNA
Windy Arbour,
Dublin 14.

Chapter NINE

Heineken cup 2011, Temple Street Children's hospital

Leinster Rugby won the Heineken cup in 2011 in dramatic fashion. They were down 6 - 22 at half time in the final against Northampton Saints, at the Millennium Stadium in Cardiff. Then Johnny Sexton did two things: he gave a talk in the dressing room at half-time which, according to the folklore, made all his team mates sit up and get ready for serious action after the restart, and he went out himself in the second half and scored two tries, three conversions, and two penalties, for a total of 22 points, to put Leinster in the lead at the end of the game, with 33 points against Northampton's 22. In other words, Northampton had no scores at all in the second half.

Sexton was man of the match on that occasion, but the captain was Brian O'Driscoll. When the Leinster team got home they made a visit to Temple Street children's hospital to show the young patients the Heineken Cup. The picture below was taken on the occasion. I was moved to comment.

Winning smile: rugby star finds a new fan at Temple Street

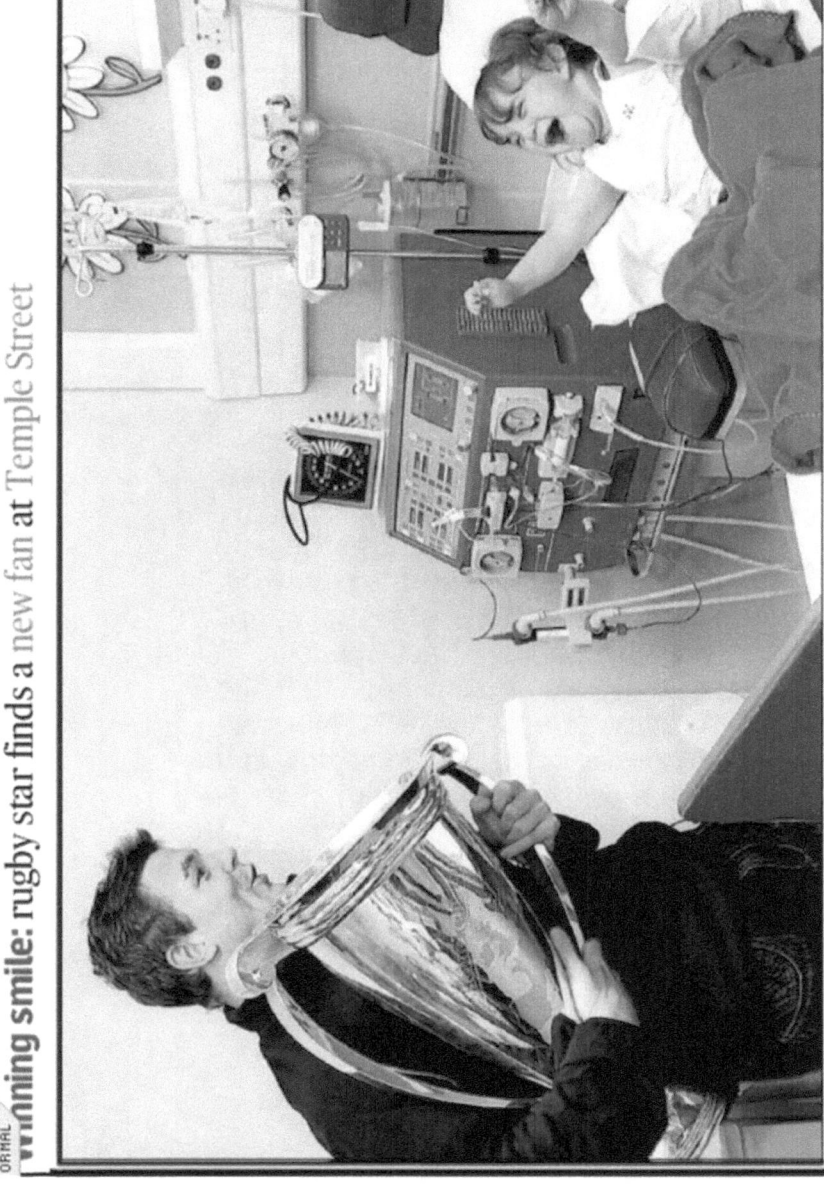

Leinster rugby player Brian O'Driscoll shows off the Heineken Cup to Michaela Morley (6), from Mayo, a young patient at the Children's University Hospital in Temple Street, Dublin. Photograph: Shane O'Neill/Fennells

THE IRISH TIMES
24-28 TARA STREET, DUBLIN 2
WEDNESDAY, JUNE 1ST, 2011

Following O'Driscoll's lead

Madam, – Brian O'Driscoll has done a lot for the nation, but the happiness and enthusiasm on the face of the little girl (Michaela Morley) in Temple Street children's hospital (Front page photograph, May 31st), brings home better than anything else the true value of the team effort that he, more than anyone, always reminds us is behind his achievements.

Is it too much to hope that the country might take a message from this: forget the carping and point-scoring, and get all citizens work together to resuscitate the country? We've been shown the model for resourcefulness, self-belief and sheer staying power. – Yours, etc,
  SEAMUS McKENNA,
Farrenboley Park,
Windy Arbour,
Dublin 14.

Chapter TEN

Orla Tinsley

Orla Tinsley wrote an article in the Irish Times of May 22nd 2007. They are a Cystic Fibrosis sufferer, and have been since they were a baby. CF is a lifelong illness, but life expectancy for victims of it can be short. At the time they wrote the article they were aged 20. They were able to tell us that, in Ireland, they could expect to live one more year. In the UK they could be around until they were 33, and in the USA until they were in their late forties. As they said, in Ireland, "We have the highest instance of CF in the world, with Third World facilities."

Their article detailed the horrors of having to go to hospital with her condition, where facilities for CF sufferers are such that they, just out of their teens, were forced to share space with elderly, senile, and psychiatric patients, so that each of them was put in danger of infection. They told of how having their iPad stolen, on top of having suffered nine consecutive sleepless nights, led to their decision to check themselves out of hospital.

Orla published their hospital diary in the Irish Times on October 14th of 2008. At that time there were eight single en-suite beds in St. Vincent's hospital, where they were. There was talk, including from a former government junior minister for health, of more beds with proper facilities for CF patients being on the way, but then those promises were forgotten about.

Facilities in Ireland for CF patients have improved since I wrote the following letters, and these improvements must owe a lot to the campaigning work done by Orla Tinsley.

THE IRISH TIMES

24-28 Tara Street, Dublin 2
Friday, May 25th, 2007

Lives in politicians' hands

Madam, – Articulate, passionate and supremely courageous are words that come to mind to describe Orla Tinsley. Deplorable, shameful and overwhelmingly depressing are reactions to reading about the punishment she has had to endure for being a victim of cystic fibrosis in the Republic of Ireland. – Yours, etc,
   SEAMUS McKENNA,
   Farrenboley Park,
   Windy Arbour,
   Dublin 14.

THE IRISH TIMES

24-28 TARA STREET, DUBLIN 2

Thursday October 16th 2008

Orla Tinsley's hospital diary

Madam, – Thank you for carrying the diary of Orla Tinsley (Opinion & Analysis, October 14th). It would make the stones weep. And then angry. Angry at the imbeciles who clog up A&E departments because they drink too much; angry at whatever bureaucracy and/or vested interest is holding up proper reform of the health service; and angry at gombeen politicians who play games with people's expectations, for example by making casual announcements of non-existent plans for specialist units. – Yours, etc,

SEAMUS McKENNA,
Farrenboley Park,
Windy Arbour,
Dublin 14.

In 2018, when they were 30, Orla Tinsley had a double lung transplant in New York. They wrote a long and heartfelt article about it in the Irish Times on Saturday Sept 15th of that year. The article was a perfectly balanced piece, coming from someone who was on the brink of death, but who had the courage and support to decide to continue to live.

Colm Tóibín's phrase "embrace of love" has a prominent part to play in it. I thought Orla Tinsley, and this article, was an inspiration.

THE IRISH TIMES

24-28 TARA STREET, DUBLIN 2
Wednesday, September 19th, 2018
irishtimes.com

Orla Tinsley – profile in courage

Sir, – What can we say about Orla Tinsley except to applaud the courage, resilience, deep humanity and never-failing positivity shown by her ("It was important to live, even though I was dying", September 15th). – Yours, etc,
   SEAMUS McKENNA,
   Windy Arbour, Dublin 14.

Cystic Fibrosis; the terrible condition

Orla Tinsley suffers from cystic fibrosis. This terrible condition also affects a greater number of people per head of the population in Ireland than it does in any other developed country. Orla has done great work in showing us all what is means to have CS, but their courage and tenacity have also highlighted the totally inadequate performances of various governments when it comes to doing something about it. I wrote about this on April 7th 2009.

THE IRISH TIMES
Tuesday, April 7, 2009
Letters

Cystic fibrosis unit funding

Madam, – Ireland has something to be ashamed of. It's not that we're ending up with a dysfunctional economy, having participated, along with the rest of the developed world, in the excesses of the Noughties. It's not because we're now wallowing in an orgy of self-pity because the chickens have come home to roost. It's not even because we cannot seem to get our priorities right in an economic downturn.

It is because we came through an era of plenty and, during that time, we did not do our duty, as a nation, to the vulnerable and the people with little power in our community. We did not do enough for education, particularly primary education. We failed to provide adequate support for the people in our midst who are the carers of dependent relatives. And head and shoulders above all else is the reprehensible manner in which our cystic fibrosis sufferers have been treated.

How a nation treats its minorities and its defenceless citizens is what determines its right to call itself civilised. The Republic, in this generation, is found seriously wanting in this regard. – Yours, etc,

SEAMUS McKENNA,
Farrenboley Park,
Windy Arbour,
Dundrum, Dublin 14.

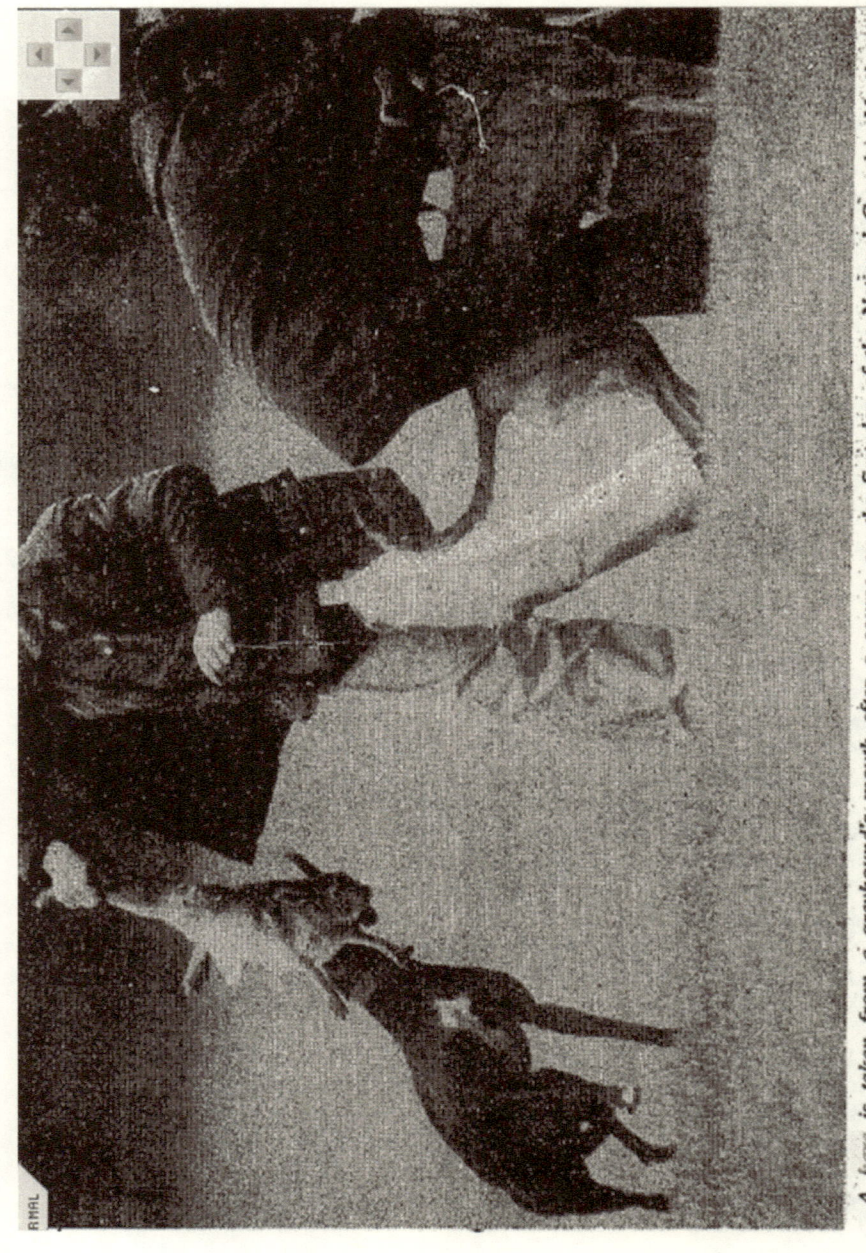

A hare is taken from a greyhound's mouth after a course on the first day of the National Coursing Meeting at Tipperary, yesterday. — (Photograph: Jack McManus; report: Sam McAughtry; page 2: page 5).

Chapter ELEVEN

Hare coursing

The photograph above was published on the front page of the Irish Times on February 1st 1983. A number of people wrote to the editor complaining about it. In all, there were a total of seven letters published in the first three weeks of the month. The first two objected to the picture being shown, although the second of these did object also to blood sports. Then writers began to see the sense and even the necessity of publishing such a picture, in order to bring the cruelty to a wider audience in the hope that something might be done about it. One writer asserted that the Irish Times "…was up to its old trick – contriving to boost its letters page…". Today, what that correspondent was complaining about would be called trolling. The term had not been invented, but it shows that a suspicion that the practice might be indulged in was, even then, in people's minds.

Mine was the last letter in the series "Hare's plight" to be published.

One man who has been consistent in the letters page on the barbarity of blood sports in general, and of hare coursing in particular, has been John FitzGerald, of Callan in Co. Kilkenny. He has been published on the subject on many, many occasions over the years.

In 1993 a law was passed specifying that greyhounds must be muzzled where the coursing takes place in an enclosure with an escape route for the hare, and in 2015 the same rule was put in place where the hare is coursed in an open field.

THE IRISH TIMES

13 D'OLIER STREET, DUBLIN 2
FRIDAY, FEBRUARY 18, 1983

HARE'S PLIGHT

Sir, — It seems that there are two types of blood sports objector. Those who object on the grounds of cruelty and those who object to being disturbed by the facts.

A number of letter writers in the last few days would fall into the latter category. Are we to conclude that they have no objection provided that pictures of the hare being dismembered are kept off the pages of *The Irish Times*? — Yours, etc..

SEAMUS McKENNA,
Findrum,
Convoy,
Co Donegal.

Chapter TWELVE

Joke of the week

From the time of the effective elimination of interest rates after the collapse of the Iron Curtain in 1989, up to the economic crash of 2008, banks all over the world had been making irresponsible loans to companies and individuals. Ireland was right up there with the worst offenders in this regard.

The rot started when buccaneering property developers found there was a welcome for them in certain fringe banks. These institutions believed they had a fool-proof formula for making larger and larger loans. It was based on three criteria: the customers borrowed to purchase assets that could be sold in the event of default of the loans, and the title deeds to these assets recorded the bank's interest in them; the customers had the ability to repay the loans independently; and they were prepared to give recourse to the bank in the event of non-performance. This last meant that the bank would only give loans to companies or individuals that had a net worth that would make it a realistic proposition for the bank to sue them when and if all else failed. Many were the PowerPoint presentations that had as their final slide one that indicated that Security plus Ability to Repay plus Recourse equalled Risk-Free Lending.

Then lenders started to bend the rules. In the case of sub-prime mortgages, for example, which were brought into being so that more so-called CDOs, or Collateralised Debt Obligations (a form of investment vehicle that could be marketed independently of the loan), could be manufactured, mortgage borrowers were no longer required to show that they had the ability to repay; the value of the asset was regarded as sufficient protection for the lending institution. In these cases, of course, recourse was impossible, because your typical sub-prime mortgage applicant, by definition, had no material wealth of any sort.

Around about the time that these things were happening, the western world found itself in a seemingly endless economic upturn. In Ireland this became known as the Celtic Tiger era. Nothing, it seemed, could go wrong. The established banks now felt that the fringe banks had been eating their lunch for long enough, and decided to emulate their more flamboyant competitors. They started to cultivate the property developers.

The biggest fallacy in the argument that Security, Ability to Repay, and Recourse together provided total safety in bank lending lay in the fact that, in a great many cases, your typical borrower had a portfolio of property assets to underly and define their net worth. It became the case that each of the factors in the equation, especially Security and Recourse, were themselves utterly dependant on property values. Now things began to look a bit incestuous. Once property went into decline the formula was seen to carry the seeds of its own destruction.

When the collapse came one of the biggest losers was Allied Irish Bank, or AIB. It became necessary for the government to make money available so that it would not go out of business altogether. The ultimate provider of these funds, of course, was the Irish taxpayer. Then, in 2010, it was announced that AIB was to be fined €2 million for overcharging customers. I thought that was a bit of a joke.

THE IRISH TIMES

24-28 TARA STREET, DUBLIN 2
MONDAY, DECEMBER 27TH 2010

Overcharging customers

Madam, – Your headline "Allied Irish Banks fined record €2 million for overcharging customers" (Finance, December 22nd) has to qualify, at least, as joke of the week. The €2 million must be paid from funding that has been made available to the bank by Irish taxpayers. The very same people who were overcharged, joined by those who had nothing at all to do with this particular institution. – Yours, etc,

SEAMUS McKENNA,
Farrenboley Park,
Windy Arbour, Dublin 14.

Chapter THIRTEEN

The financial crisis of 2008

An unpleasant precedent

During the chaotic times that prevailed in the wake of the global financial crisis, which started in 2008, there were many efforts made, especially at European Union level, to steady the badly holed ship that was the Eurozone banking system. Austerity measures, which included among many other things reductions in all public spending, increased taxation, and a cut in the salaries of public servants, were the order of the day. Ireland, along with Italy, Greece, Portugal, and Spain were particularly badly affected by these impositions.

But then news came through that the nation of Cyprus, which had joined the EU only in 2004, was to be selected for special treatment. All bank deposits were to be subjected to a levy. This was an unprecedented development in the EU, where bank accounts, especially those of small savers, had up to then been regarded as sacrosanct.

At the time it was speculated that this measure was aimed at Russian customers of the Cypriot banks, who accounted at the time for an eyebrow-raising one-third of all bank deposits on the non-Turkish part of the island. Russia, at that time, had not assumed the pariah state status that fell to its lot after the invasion of Ukraine, which was years in the future, so there was a lot of sympathy for Cyprus outside of the European Central Bank (ECB), the European Commission, and the International Monetary Fund (IMF), the constituent members of the so-called Troika.

So strong were the financial ties that Cyprus had with Russia that a delegation from Cyprus went to the Kremlin to attempt to garner Russian assistance in the form of a financial bail-out. It returned empty-handed.

As someone who was an enthusiastic Europhile, I was disillusioned, to say the least, by the ravishing of ordinary people's bank accounts in this way. What did I do? I wrote a letter to the editor of the Irish Times, of course. Reading over it now, I can see that my feelings were strong.

THE IRISH TIMES

24-28 TARA STREET, DUBLIN 2
Wednesday, March 20th, 2013
irishtimes.com

Controversial Cypriot 'bailout' plan

Sir, – As someone who was born not too long after the end of the second World War, the development of the EU has easily been the most significant event to have happened in this writer's lifetime. It has been welcomed on a large number of levels. Early years in the stultifying atmosphere of autocratic, priest-ridden Ireland gave EU anti-discrimination and other, similar, liberal directives the quality of large doses of refreshing, invigorating fresh air. Fiscal and monetary austerity packages have been tolerated and even welcomed as moves to impose required discipline on the irresponsible and ultimately unsustainable economic models that prevailed prior to the great financial crisis.

But now, at last, Homer has well and truly nodded. Gestures of approval while watching Mario Draghi pronouncing that the "Sovereign signature remains a pillar of stability" when explaining that it was impossible to renege on guarantees that had been given to bank bondholders by the Irish government, no matter how unfortunate they have turned out to be in hindsight, have now turned into gasps of dismay at the idea that a collective punishment is to be visited on ordinary Cypriots who believed that their assets were safe in an institution that formed part of the eurozone banking system.

This is indeed a retrograde step. It is the opening of a door that will never be capable of being closed. It is an invitation for all, whether native Europeans or those who are here as our guests, to believe that no bank account, anywhere in the euro zone, is now safe from the depredations of those in authority who would invade their private, up-to-now sacrosanct assets. Contagion is too weak a word to describe the prospects that have now reared their ugly heads.

We have not heard the end of this. – Yours, etc,
SEAMUS McKENNA,
Farrenboley Park,
Windy Arbour, Dublin 14.

Bust and austerity

The government tried to undo the damage that had been inflicted on the country by the financial crisis, but by the end of 2010 it was obvious it needed assistance. In November it bit the bullet and invited three institutions, The International Monetary Fund, the European Central Bank, and the European Commission to come and help. This group became known as the Troika. In response of getting the kind of financial assistance that was needed to support the main Irish banks, which were on the verge of failure, and allowing life in Ireland to continue at some level of normality, the government followed the prescriptions laid down by the Troika's economists. These resulted in austerity, which hit people at all levels, but was eventually seen to be a success.

Then, in 2012, the EU proposed a Fiscal Stability Treaty, which would formalise, across the EU, the kind of balanced budgets and fiscal corrective mechanisms that were designed to ensure that a financial crisis like the one that started in 2008 could not occur again. This was opposed by the left-wing members of the opposition. Enactment of the treaty required a referendum.

I wrote the following in support.

THE IRISH TIMES

24-28 TARA STREET, DUBLIN 2
TUESDAY, MAY 29th, 2012
irishtimes.com

Preparing for European treaty vote

Sir, – Ireland now has an opportunity to get out of the so-called southern countries grouping that has been given the awful acronym PIIGS. We will do that by signing up for fiscally responsible rules that will instead associate us with the responsible, efficient, mature economies at the core.

This means voting Yes in the forthcoming referendum.

Then our representatives at the Council [of Ministers] (where the power is and where the participants have been democratically elected by the citizens of their individual countries, despite all the noise about a "democratic deficit") can confidently claim full participation in the measures that can and will be undertaken to grow the euro zone economy as a whole.

Expecting growth to be paid for by the countries that have a track record of proper financial management (Germany, The Netherlands, Finland, Austria) while the free riders of the zone continue to be facilitated in their habits is naive in the extreme, and it is irresponsible of the Irish left to represent to the people that anything other than disciplined fiscal management is a practical proposition within the euro zone.

Outside of it is another matter entirely – that way lies utter chaos, especially for a small, open economy like ours in a globalised marketplace.

I will be voting Yes. – Yours, etc,
SEAMUS MCKENNA,
Farrenboley Park,
Windy Arbour, Dublin 14.

Recovery

The recovery did come, of course. The people from the IMF, the European Central Bank and the Commission all went back home, leaving the Irish economy in good shape, albeit in somewhat reduced circumstances from what it was like immediately before the crash.

Olli Rehn was the European commissioner for economic and monetary affairs, and José Manuel Barroso was the president of the European Commission. Many people in Ireland held those two responsible for the austerity measures that had to be endured in order to recover from the melt down in the economy. There was a suggestion in a news report that they would not be welcome at a ceremony to celebrate our completion of the recovery programme. I thought this was wrong:

THE IRISH TIMES

24-28 TARA STREET, DUBLIN 2
Tuesday, December 17th, 2013
irishtimes.com

Sir, – How sad and depressing to read a headline that says Ollie Rehn and Manuel Borroso were "told to stay away" from events to mark our exit from the programme of recovery which, with the involvement of the IMF, was facilitated by EU institutions (Front page, December 14th).

Instead of insulting the very people who saved our bacon, the Government's impulse should have been to do the direct opposite. This was a good chance to remind the Irish public that, bad as things have been and still are, it is easy to demonstrate that they would have been a whole lot worse without the assistance of our friends in Europe.

If, instead of having to follow the precepts of responsible and prudent central Europeans, with copious loans from the same source to make sure that state wages and other expenses, including social welfare, could still be paid in the interim, we were left to the dictates of the markets as a bankrupt country, we would have been shown what true hardship entails.

The people of Ukraine can see the truth of the matter. A quote from one of the pro-EU protesters in Kiev in the same edition of your paper says "We know it's not paradise in the EU. But it gives hope for a better life. That's why we are here". – Yours, etc,
SEAMUS McKENNA,
Farrenboley Park,
Windy Arbour,
Dublin 14.

The austerity measures were traumatic for many in Ireland. As late as 2017 there were still letters in the paper about it. I sent in this one, which was published:

THE IRISH TIMES

24-28 TARA STREET, DUBLIN 2
Monday, July 10th, 2017
irishtimes.com

A bailout in an hour of need

Sir, – Donal McGrath has a flawed understanding of what forced austerity is, in his castigation of the EU for its role in Ireland's bailout ("A bailout in an hour of need", July 7th). Ireland was not forced to do anything at that time. Instead it agreed to conditions that were laid down in return for keeping the lights on, our teachers, nurses, police, firefighters and civil servants paid a substantial amount of their pre-austerity salaries, and our State (as opposed to private) pensions maintained. Forced austerity is when a nation runs out of money to the extent that it cannot do any of those things, as happened in Argentina in 2001.

The poor quality of the argument made by Mr McGrath is further illustrated by the fact that he feels it necessary to bring forward something that might or might not happen in the future ("probably at the cost of another round of austerity") in order to bolster it. – Yours, etc,
SEAMUS McKENNA,
Windy Arbour,
Dublin 14.

Chapter FOURTEEN

Science in the island of saints and scholars

Since the activities of the IDA (Industrial Development Authority), and other agencies that have the job of promoting quality job creation in Ireland, began to bear fruit, and particularly now that their successes have been multiplied many times over, we do not seem to hear as much about the Island of Saints and Scholars, which is what Ireland used to be called.

The designation was well earned. Thomas Cahill, in his book "How the Irish Saved Civilisation", argues that

> "After the fall of Rome, Irish monks protected and reproduced the written artifacts of Rome, preserving many concepts of Roman civilization and actively continuing the spread of Christianity. They copied thousands of manuscripts that served as the repositories for Greco-Roman and Judeo-Christian culture. Without their work, everything that happened subsequently would have been unthinkable. Irish monks brought their uniquely Irish world-view to the task of maintaining the very record of Western civilization. The Irish church saved Christian ideas and practices that were being lost in the crumbling Empire."

Cahill gives a special place to St Columba, who was vigorous in his work of spreading Christianity through the monks he trained and the monasteries he set up.

So it would appear that the Saints and Scholars appellation was well earned. But in modern times there is a problem, and it is this: the religious idea that everything on Earth has emanated from, and is governed by, a supreme, supernatural being, clashes head-on with the principles of science. The scientific method demands that investigators have no preconceived idea about how something works. Divine revelation, which is the basis of Christianity, can have no part in scientific enquiry. If an hypothesis, when tested, is found to be inconsistent with the evidence then it must be changed, or abandoned completely. There can be no exceptions. To do anything else is to repudiate science.

THE IRISH TIMES

24-28 TARA STREET, DUBLIN 2
THURSDAY, JANUARY 19TH, 2012

Making Ireland 'the place of science'

Sir, – David McConnell's excellent letter on science (January 17th) is a breath of fresh air. Of course science should be cultivated for more than the potential for job creation that it holds. Scientific inquiry opens up the prospect of beautiful and deeply satisfying experiences, and there is no better place to start with this than in the study of Darwinian evolution, as proposed by Prof McConnell.

His call for rationality, however, will require a rethink about the way our primary schools, in particular, are managed. As long as we have the so-called integrated curriculum, which infuses Catholic doctrine into all school subjects in the 90 per cent or more of our national primary schools that are under the management of the church, we will have a direct conflict in the minds of our young people. How can they be expected to reconcile the certainty of religious doctrine with the idea of a scientific theory, which can never be absolutely proven and which the scientific method only allows to be disproven or modified?

How can we match, for example, the laws of thermodynamics with accounts of miracles and the existence of esoteric entities such as the immortal soul, which are given to impressionable children as indisputable facts by those they are taught to understand are in a position of authority? This particular elephant in the room will have to be confronted, and the sooner the better. – Yours, etc,

SEAMUS McKENNA,
Farrenboley Park,
Windy Arbour,
Dublin 14.

Chapter FIFTEEN

General election 2011

After the economic crash of 2008 the ruling parties in Ireland must have been anticipating the next general election with trepidation. Fianna Fáil, in particular, the anchor in the coalition government, was widely portrayed in opinion and news media as the real villain of the piece, given its cosy relations with the bankers, property developers, and assorted other speculators that were perceived to have been the baddies that had brought about the collapse.

And they were correct. Fianna Fáil was practically wiped out. From being the largest single political party, with the prospect at one stage of forming a government on its own, it fell to third largest after Fine Gael and Labour, who were now the largest and second largest respectively.

Fine Gael reaped the benefits from the fallout. Its leader, Enda Kenny, found himself elected Taoiseach (Prime Minister), an outcome that seemed to surprise even himself. Prior to the election, in an attempt to copper-fasten the result, he gave an interview to the Irish Catholic newspaper, the content of which would have been aimed at his supporters in what is a religiously conservative part of the country, Co. Mayo. He undertook not to legislate for abortion, which the government was required to do because of the finding by the European Court of Human Rights, earlier that year, that the Irish state was in violation of article 8 of the European Convention on Human Rights, because there was no clarity in Ireland about the circumstances under which a woman could get an abortion.

In the event, Enda Kenny grew into the job, and made many strong interventions in his position as Prime Minister. Perhaps the most notable of these was when the excoriated the Catholic Church over the way it facilitated the cover up of child sexual abuse. He did this from his position of privilege in the Dáil.

THE IRISH TIMES

24-28 TARA STREET, DUBLIN 2

Friday December 18th 2007

European court ruling on abortion

Madam, – Who does Enda Kenny think he is, giving an undertaking to a Catholic newspaper that his Fine Gael party will not legislate for abortion if it is voted into power (Front page, December 17th). It is time he and politicians like him are made to understand that when they are elected they represent all the people of the state and not just one sectional grouping, no matter how large it is. – Yours, etc,
SEAMUS McKENNA,
Farrenboley Park,
Windy Arbour,
Dublin 14.

Chapter FIFTEEN

Gun violence in the USA

Guns are ubiquitous in the United States. This is as a result of the Second Amendment to the Constitution, which confers on adult citizens the right to bear arms. When this amendment was ratified, as part of the Bill of Rights, the USA was not long in being; the amendment was made in 1791, some fifteen years after the Declaration of Independence. Memories of the part played by local militia in the War of Independence were strong, and the rulers of the various states of the new union were still wary of being interfered with by a federal government. Thus the wording of the amendment is significant:

> "A well regulated Militia, being necessary to the security of a free State, the right of the people to keep and bear Arms, shall not be infringed."

The framers wanted their supporters to be already armed in the event that it might be necessary to call on them for defensive action. In addition, to be armed was seen as necessary for self-defence or the defence of one's family. This right actually followed on from the terms of the English Bill of Rights of 1689, when the right to bear arms was confined to Protestants, and was seen as part of the natural right of resistance and self-preservation, "…when the sanctions of society and laws are found insufficient to restrain the violence of oppression," according to the Justice of the Court of the King's Bench at the time.

None of this, of course, could take any account of the developments that have taken place in the design and manufacture of firearms since these sentiments were current. The Second Amendment is now vigorously defended by powerful organisations in the US, of which the most notable is the National Rifle Association, or NRA. But they seem to be oblivious to the suffering that is caused, almost every day, because the most powerful weapons and ammunition are allowed to get into the hands of very sick individuals, almost without restraint.

When my letter was published the latest atrocity to be reported on was a mass killing in the Sandy Hook elementary school, in Newtown, Connecticut. There, in 2012, a single individual killed twenty children between the ages of six and seven, as well as six of their teachers. He then shot and killed himself. He had murdered his own mother before he went on his rampage.

The Washington Post reported that in the same year there had been a total of sixteen similar shooting in the US, which had resulted in the deaths of at least 88 people, and had left many more seriously injured.

This letter was one of the few that attained what I came to regard as pole position in the letters page of the paper: the first letter to be printed, defined as the one that appeared in the top left-hand location on the page.

Lessons from Sandy Hook

Sir, – When I bought a bottle of water at half-time in the recent Leinster/Clermont Auvergne game, the barman removed the top and retained it. He did this, not because he suspected me of being the kind of person who would be tempted to throw it at someone, but because the stadium has made this a regulation to deny certain individuals the ability to do exactly that.

Therefore, I had to pay a small price (the danger that the water would spill before I could drink it) for the tendency of others to behave badly.

Although I would like to be able to do target practice with a high-powered rifle, I understand that I cannot do so in this country, for the same reason.

It is time it was borne in on our American friends that if they could get around the blind spot that afflicts them regarding gun control, and pay the small price this would require in terms of personal liberties, they would make a move towards denying some deeply disturbed individuals the ability to create enormous anguish and suffering in their communities. – Yours, etc,

SEAMUS McKENNA,
Farrenboley Park,
Windy Arbour, Dublin 14.

Chapter SIXTEEN

Why the Celtic Tiger took so long to arrive

In a well-received article in the Irish Times of October 24th., 2006, the writer and academic, Declan Kiberd, dissected what his sub-editor called "Our epic journey to affluence."
    He was critical of the educational regime that had existed in the years after independence, when Ireland's culture had prospered, and its politicians had produced one of the first anti-imperial movements of the 20th century, but at the cost of the neglect of the kind of practical education that would prepare the people for the coming of technology and manufacture. He deplored the fact that, even in the 1960s, the brightest students were set to study Latin, while the less-gifted "did something called commerce."
    I had just read what I still regard as a great book by then Professor of Politics at University College, Dublin (UCD), Dr. Tom Garvin. It had left me in no doubt about reasons why Ireland lagged all other developed nations for so long in the area of economic growth.

Why the Celtic Tiger took so long to arrive

Madam, – It is hard to believe that Declan Kiberd could attempt to answer the question of why the coming of the Celtic Tiger took so long without mentioning the stultifying alliance in the earlier years of this State between a power-crazed Catholic Hierarchy and a rabidly nationalistic rump in the elected and administrative authorities.

Both put their own dogma and extreme conservatism way above the economic or social interests of the people, placing severe restrictions on mass education, for instance.

Mr Kiberd wants to know why economics took a century to catch up with culture and politics.

Well, while Ireland's entrepreneurs were escaping to the US, Australia, Canada, the UK and many other places, so too were many of its writers, musicians, painters and playwrights. But even when based in Paris or Vienna, James Joyce *et al.* remained Irish authors, while the Chuck Feeneys of the world were visible only in the economies of their adopted countries, at least until recently.

The politicians, unfortunately, stayed at home.

For a lot more on this topic, readers (and Mr Kiberd) should see Tom Garvin's book *Preventing the Future: Why was Ireland so poor for so long?* – Yours, etc,

SEAMUS McKENNA,
Farrenboley Park,
Windy Arbour,
Dublin 14.

Chapter SEVENTEEN

Would Fianna Fáil survive?

As can be seen in other letters in this collection, there was even more interest than there otherwise would have been, in a country where politics is a very popular spectator sport, in the general election of 2011, because it was the first one to take place after the economic meltdown that started in 2008 (see also 'General election 2011" above).

All the opinion polls had it that the incumbent government, led by Fianna Fáil, would suffer badly because it was being blamed for the damage that was inflicted during the economic crisis. Elements of the history of that party were invoked by many letter writers, including your humble servant, and other opinion contributors. One man who had indulged in trenchant criticism of the Soldiers of Destiny, as FF was at one stage pleased to style itself, was Conor Cruise O'Brien, himself a colourful individual and an acerbic commentor. He had served as Editor-in-Chief of the Observer newspaper, based in London, among many other roles, including that of a government minister.

O'Brien had a particular animus for Charles J. Haughey, one of the Fianna Fáil's more controversial leaders. For example, it was O'Brien who coined the word GUBU, after the utterances of Haughey when he was interviewed on TV in the wake of the Malcolm McArthur affair, when a double murderer on the run was found hiding in the apartment of Haughey's Attorney General during the term of one of his governments.

Haughey had said, with some validity, that this happenstance was Grotesque, Unbelievable, Bizarre, Unprecedented. O'Brien made a new term from the acronym of this phrase, and placed it in the Hiberno-English lexicon. It means a chaotic mess, particularly one that involves politics or politicians. Then, in 1982, after one of Haughey's occasional electoral defeats, O'Brien wrote the immortal phrase that began with "… if I were to see Mr. Haughey buried at midnight at a crossroads, with a stake driven through his heart – politically speaking…"

You can read the rest of this quote in the letter below.

THE IRISH TIMES

24-28 TARA STREET, DUBLIN 2
TUESDAY, FEBRUARY 1ST, 2011
irishtimes.com

Preparing for the general election

Madam, – Although it is hard to agree totally with John Waters when he seems to suggest that there's a little bit of Fianna Fáil in all of us here in Ireland, his piece (Opinion, Janurary 28th) does provide food for thought.

In the run-up to the election we'd do well to consider that the words written by Conor Cruise O'Brien in the *Observer* in 1982, in relation to an iconic Fianna Fáil character, might just as easily apply to the party of which that gentleman was once the leader: "If I saw Mr Haughey buried at midnight at a crossroads, with a stake driven through his heart – politically speaking – I should continue to wear a clove of garlic round my neck, just in case". – Yours, etc,
SEAMUS MCKENNA,
Farrenboley Park,
Windy Arbour, Dublin 14.

Chapter EIGHTEEN

Clamping at the tram terminus carpark

She drove her car from home to the tram terminus. It was too far to walk. She'd use the Park & Ride facility. That'd mean a parking charge. It will be paid. Her car will have a parking permit ticket on it. She's always been thoroughly law abiding in regard to things like this.

But what's this? There are no parking permit tickets anymore. The usual thing when parking is that you Park and Display. Everyone knows how that works. You get the little slip that records the time you've arrived, display it above the dashboard of your car so that roaming inspectors can see it (if they don't see a ticket you get clamped) and then pay for whatever time you've been there when you get back to the car and are ready to leave.

But now they have a new system. The tram company has decided to outsource the whole thing to a high-tech car clamping company. What you do now is you key your car registration number into the machine, and go on your way. The car parking regulators come along with a hand-held scanner that's linked wirelessly to the machine. If they scan your plate and its not in the database, then you get clamped.

Every writer knows how easy it is to make a typo. They're so common they're regarded as something that happens, gets caught and corrected (or not), and all without the slightest apportioning of blame to the person who made it. That is, of course, unless you happen to travel on the Dublin tram system known as the LUAS.

THE IRISH TIMES

24-28 TARA STREET, DUBLIN 2
Wednesday, January 2nd, 2019
irishtimes.com

Clampers and drivers

Sir, – Your report on the intervention of the Minister for Transport in the case where a woman's car was clamped at the Luas carpark in Stillorgan, Co Dublin, is replete with references to "statutory periods", "clamping appeals officer", the Vehicle Clamping Act 2015 and, of course, thinly veiled outrage that the Minister got involved in this matter at all ("Shane Ross 'strongly asked' for constituent's clamping fine to be reconsidered", News, December 29th).

The woman concerned had mistyped her car registration when paying for her parking. A friend of mine, also female, suffered very badly in the same car park when she transposed two numbers of her car registration at the parking payment machine. She was left isolated late at night in an otherwise deserted area for a substantial period of time, with her car immobilised, until the de-clamping unit arrived. The fee she had to pay for that was a trivial matter in comparison to the trauma she had suffered up to that point.

That's the real news in these cases. The people concerned were not penalised for failing to pay for parking. They received a severe and totally disproportionate punishment for nothing worse than making a typographical error. And despite all the responses from the National Transport Authority (NTA) about the appeals process and so forth, the relevant Act says nothing at all about the onus being placed on drivers to record their car registrations at parking-ticket machines.

It is high time that this grossly unfair method of administering parking was stopped. It is in this regard that the Minister could make a real contribution.
– Yours, etc,
SEAMUS McKENNA,
Windy Arbour,
Dublin 14.

Chapter TWENTY

Ireland's approach to public service transportation

This particular regular flier always took the Blue Coach in from Dublin airport on trips home from a posting in Brussels in the early years of this century. What is now known as the Aircoach service was then in its infancy.

A traveller on a well-worn route to anywhere picks up certain preferences, and in this case mine was to make sure that I was sitting just behind and to the left of the driver. I never spoke to him, but I could overhear, on a clear channel, his interactions with other customers, and even with himself when, for example, he would speak his thoughts out loud on the behaviour of other road users:

"You might as well have the whole car in the bus lane as two of the wheels."

The drivers had a good relationship with regular users of the service, many of whom were in the livery of one or other of the airlines.

In 2012 a letter appeared from another writer complaining about the unreliable information displays on the DART (Dublin Area Rapid Transport) train system, and the difficulties that this might cause for tourists. I decided to let readers know of my experiences. I wasn't over enamoured of the heading the letters editor chose for my effort on this occasion but, hey, as my American friends might say, I got published.

THE IRISH TIMES

24-28 TARA STREET, DUBLIN 2
THURSDAY, JUNE 28TH, 2012
irishtimes.com

Ah shure, isn't it Ireland?

Sir, – Padraig O'Rourke has a point about the dodgy information displays on the Dart (June 27th), and their impact on our many visitors from abroad, but I wouldn't make too much of it.

About 14 years ago I had occasion to use the, excellent, "blue bus" service to and from Dublin Airport on a regular basis. The driver had to call out the stops himself without benefit of amplification, which led to something of a rapport developing between him and his passengers. This led to him obliging certain people who wanted to be dropped off at intermediate, unofficial points. On one occasion an American inquired how near we were to where he was going, and was told it was the next stop. Then another passenger needed to use an impromptu one. The door opened, the American came forward but the driver caught him in time and set him right.

"But I thought you said mine was the next stop?" There was the slightest of pauses from the driver before he said: "I meant the next official stop".

We all loved this kind of thing; not least the Americans. You got the feeling that it was what they expected, and it constituted, in fact, the material for the stories they would dine out on when they got home. – Yours, etc,
SEAMUS MCKENNA,
Farrenboley Park,
Windy Arbour,
Dublin 14.

Chapter TWENTY ONE

Psychology and belief

In days gone by, before the development of psychiatric medicine and counselling, it was often believed that people who suffered from conditions such as depression, epilepsy, schizophrenia, and other mental illnesses, were possessed by the devil. The religious response to this was the practice of exorcism, where a priest would perform rites over the effected person in an attempt to expel the "evil spirits".

Many ancient procedures, for example bloodletting, or the draining of the blood from a patient in an attempt to cure illness or disease, have been discredited and are no longer used in the developed world. Exorcism surely falls into that category. At the very least it must have the effect of delaying the point at which the patient is brought for appropriate professional medical treatment.

An article in Psychology Today, published in the USA in 2011, seemed to suggest that exorcism might have a part to play in the calming of very disturbed people in order to make them amenable to treatment by a psychiatrist, but only if the patient is a religious believer to begin with. My problem with this kind of rationale is that it is likely to be pounced upon by apologists for religion as an endorsement of the idea that exorcism works.

On October 9th 2018, an article appeared in the Irish Times which said that the Catholic Bishop of Waterford and Lismore had announced in a radio interview that he was setting up a team to carry out exorcisms. The comments attributed to the bishop might have come straight out of the screenplay for the movie The Exorcist. The following is an extract from the report.

> 'He said he had never seen an exorcism himself. "But I have certainly felt the presence of evil," he said. "I remember one particular priest, a friend of mine who I knew who was involved in one particular case, and it was a girl, a professional girl, young, who came with her mother, and there were four men, kind of rugby types, to hold her down in the chair, such strength she had.
>
> "The priest had warned the four guys beforehand: just make sure you've gone to Confession and one guy didn't go to Confession, one of the four, and the girl with a voice that wasn't hers, it was a male voice coming out of her, actually called out the sins of your man, the guy who hadn't gone to Confession," the bishop said.
>
> "I'm sorry if I'm scaring anybody."'

This particular bishop is a member of the right-wing Catholic organisation, Opus Dei, according to Patsy McGarry, while reviewing the book 'Opus' by Gareth Gore in the Irish Times of Oct 21 2024. It is well known that this secretive organisation has been active behind the scenes in supporting the US presidential ambitions of one Donald Trump, and the manner in which that individual was responsible for packing the US Supreme Court with judges who would be amenable to a deeply conservative interpretation of the US Constitution, especially in relation to women's rights.

Opus Dei, of course, was also referenced by Dan Brown in his book, 'The Da Vinci Code'. Many senior Catholic churchmen were outraged by what Brown portrayed there, forgetting that it was a work of fiction, and a flawed one at that. Perhaps if the church encourages organisations that trade in secrecy and political skullduggery, then it should expect to come to the attention of the Dan Browns of this world.

THE IRISH TIMES

24-28 TARA STREET, DUBLIN 2
Thursday, October 11th, 2018
irishtimes.com

Exorcism and ministry

Sir, – At the end of your report, the bishop is quoted as saying that he was sorry if he was scaring anybody. My feelings were much stronger than that. They ranged from incredulity, that a grown man could be so gullible in this day and age, to outrage when I considered that this individual has the patronage of the great majority of our taxpayer-funded schools within the borders of his diocese. – Yours, etc,
　　SEAMUS McKENNA,
　Windy Arbour,
　Dublin 14.

Chapter TWENTY ONE

United States politics

The accession of Barack Obama

The President of the United States is effectively the leader of the western world. Who gets to hold that office is of concern to citizens of other countries, even if they do not have a vote in the matter.

The first letter I had in the Irish Times on this topic concerned Barack Obama. It was a somewhat tongue-in-cheek effort, aimed at someone who held religiously-motivated conservative views about what should be in the laws of the land, who nevertheless appeared to welcome the election of Obama, a man well-known, even then, for his liberal outlook.

THE IRISH TIMES

Letters

Burden of hope on Barack Obama

Fri Jan 09 2009 - 00:00

Madam, – The expectations surrounding the accession, later this month, of Barack Obama to the presidency of the United States are just a little bit worrying. A significant proportion of the global financial industry is relying on him for a solution to the recession. We're hearing a lot about what he's going to do about both Iran and Iraq and there seems to be a perception that if he were to break his self-imposed silence regarding the Gaza Strip, that too might be resolved.

Now we have Kathy Sinnott MEP telling The Irish Times (January 7th) that, having checked with people in the US, the "feeling seems to be that the situation [regarding possible new US legislation on abortion] will be defused by President Obama".

All in all it might appear that Mr Obama is being cast in the role of saviour of the world. Quite a big ask, as they say. The concern is that any shortfall in fulfilling these elevated hopes might have a prejudicial effect on what has the hallmark of quite a competent presidency. – Yours, etc,

SEAMUS McKENNA,
Farrenboley Park,
Windy Arbour,
Dublin 14.

Leo Varadkar in the USA for St. Patrick's Day

Every year Ireland gets to have unique access to the holders of the White House and other very important people in American politics. In 2018 it was the turn of then Taoiseach, Leo Varadkar, to present the traditional bowl of shamrock to the President, and to make a speech.

Over the years this tradition has been of enormous value to Ireland. It started as a political sop to the large Irish diaspora in the US, and got a fantastic boost during the John F. Kennedy administration. It has been further bolstered by Joe Biden, who has made no secret of the fact that he is extremely proud of his Irish roots.

On the occasion of Varadkar's speech in 2018 Fintan O'Toole took it upon himself to object to the idea that US values might also correspond with Irish values, as had been claimed by the Taoiseach in his speech. It was one of the few occasions I found that I had to take Fintan O'Toole to task, but in fairness to him he might have written what he did as a reaction to some of the policies and decision made by the US President at the time, Donald Trump.

Trump knew Ireland too. He owned a golf course and conference centre in Co. Clare at the time of Varadkar's visit, which he had purchased in 2014.

THE IRISH TIMES

24-28 TARA STREET, DUBLIN 2
Wednesday, March 21st, 2018
irishtimes.com

Irish values and American values

Sir, – Fintan O'Toole is wide of the mark in his criticism of Leo Varadkar's speech in Washington last week ("No, Taoiseach, Irish values are not American values", Opinion & Analysis, March 20th). The Taoiseach was alluding to the historical United States, which did indeed give the world true democracy. The US revolution predated the French one, but both of them created the environment where hereditary monarchs or religious autocrats could no longer have the absolute physical and psychological power they enjoyed, and abused, up to then in Europe and further afield.

For generations, America did indeed welcome the world's huddled masses to its shores. That it is not doing so now is down to the constraints imposed by severe population growth. But we can hope that reminders of its past, of the sort provided by the Taoiseach when he, briefly but uniquely, had its leader's attention, might, just might, make it temper its current measures in the name of compassion and humanity.

The US is the parent of globalisation, and it is this, despite the headline-grabbing opposing cases, that has made the world as a whole far more integrated, tolerant, and caring than it ever had been before. – Yours, etc,

SEAMUS McKENNA
Windy Arbour,
Dublin 14.

Donald Trump

Donald Trump certainly brought out the worst in many of the people who criticised him. In September of 2018 Fintan O'Toole compared the US President to Adolf Hitler, in a article he wrote which had as its subject an Op-ed piece in the New York Times that was ostensibly written by a Trump White House staff member, which was critical of the President.

Bad idea, I thought. It has long been an unwritten rule that commentators everywhere should resist the temptation to compare anything to what happened during the Nazi regime in Germany. That particular time in history was of a scale of evil that was stupendous. To say that anything at all that has happened since bears comparison with it is to move along the road towards normalising it.

I wrote the following in response to O'Toole's article:

THE IRISH TIMES

Letters

Trump and the 'resistance'

Wed Sept 12 2018 - 00:08

Sir, – It is unwise for any commentator to make comparisons between the enormity of what happened in 1930s and 1940s Europe with anything in the western world today, and Fintan O'Toole's remarks about those who surround the current president of the US are no exception to this ("'Adults in the room' are not the resistance – they are Trump collaborators", Opinion & Analysis, September 11th).

Your columnist ignores the fact that Donald Trump, for better or worse, is the democratically elected president of a democracy that is as transparent as any that exists today, and that the constitution of the US, the provisions of which will be observed, ensures that his tenure in that office cannot exceed eight years, even if re-elected, of which 18 months have already elapsed.

One does not have to agree with Mr Trump to realise that any methodology for his removal, other than through the democratic process, would be so traumatic for global affairs that a policy of containment until he is voted out or must leave, which is what the New York Times opinion piece advocates, is the only realistic option. – Yours, etc,

SEAMUS McKENNA, Windy Arbour, Dublin 14.

Trump's visit to Ireland

In 2019 it became known that Donald Trump, in his role as President of the United States, was to visit Ireland. Naturally, any visit by a United States President was going to be welcomed. The first thing on the agenda in preparation was to establish some Irish connection with his forebears. If that was not possible then Ireland would welcome him anyway, and make him an honorary Irishman.

When Barack Obama came to Ireland as President a family in Moneygall, Co. Offaly, was identified as his Irish relatives. Obama played along, to the extent of joking that perhaps his name was really O'Bama. An Irish entrepreneur, who had made his money in hamburgers restaurants, established what he called the Barack Obama Plaza as a motorway service area in the wake of the visit. Among other things my letter, which follows, made the point that nothing similar was going to happen after Donald Trump went back to the US.

For a long time in advance of the visit, it was suggested by the White House that a meeting between the President and the Taoiseach, Leo Varadkar, should take place at Trump's golf resort in Co. Clare.

Trump's trip to Ireland

Sir, – Many commentators have interpreted a section of the Mueller report as evidence that Donald Trump never expected to win the US presidential election; that his entry into the race was nothing more than an attempt to bolster his Trump brand. That has the ring of truth about it, given his previous history.

More recently, the Trump organisation made it clear it would object strongly and legally if a prominent Irish fast-food chain used the Trump name for any of its developments, when it had already been successful in using the name of a previous US president, Barack Obama, for a similar purpose. Therefore it seems that Trump himself sees his name as a logo.

It would be wildly inappropriate for our Taoiseach to give his support to such branding. It is right that Leo Varadkar should meet US President Trump, but it is also essential that he declines any invitation that would merely be for the purposes of strengthening an already notorious corporate identity.

This means the Trump International Golf Links and Hotel at Doonbeg is ruled out as the venue for such a meeting, especially while Trump remains as US president. – Yours, etc,
SEAMUS McKENNA,
Dublin 14.

The next letter was triggered by the New York Times columnist, Maureen O'Dowd, whose articles are syndicated to The Irish Times. Ms. O'Dowd is of proud Irish heritage, and is also a committed opponent of Donald Trump.

Occasionally, in pursuit of the democratic ideals of hearing the other person's point of view, she gives her column over to her brother, who is a Trump supporter. On the occasion of the writing of this letter, it was her brother I had just read. Trump had been voted out of office at the time, but he did not go quietly. A few weeks after this letter was written his supporters, egged on by the man himself, attacked the United States Capitol building in Washington DC.

THE IRISH TIMES

24-28 TARA STREET, DUBLIN 2
Wednesday, December 2nd, 2020
irishtimes.com

'A lament for mercurial Trump'

Sir, – In 2016, when Donald Trump got elected, I had a civilised conversation with an American acquaintance who identified herself as someone who had helped to put him in power. I said that, while I would not have voted for him, now that he was in power, I recognised that he was likely to be a disruptor, and that "perhaps the system needed some disruption".

Well, we've had more than enough of that. His efforts were accompanied by a total lack of responsibility for global issues, in which the US has a deep historical stake, rank misogyny, total and absolute hypocrisy in order to garner the religious vote, and a level of bad taste that was shocking even by the standards set by certain elements of American society heretofore.

After all of that I still applaud Maureen O'Dowd's decision to let her Trumpist brother have the platform of her column ("'A brother's lament for mercurial Trump", Opinion, World, November 30th). – Yours, etc,
SEAMUS McKENNA,
Dublin 14.

Sign of spring

A lamb pictured at the Curragh in Co Kildare. Lambing season can be a very busy time on farms while sheep can be extra vulnerable during the first few months of the year

Photograph: Laura Hutton

Chapter TWENTY TWO

Seasonal lamb

When their throats were cut the blood gurgled into the drains like surface water after a thunderstorm. It was hard to believe that a body could hold so much blood. It had a slight metallic odour, to which the executioners had become inured. The people with the knives were skilled, and continued to perfect their techniques over time. They were strong enough to ensure that the work was done expeditiously.

To do it right, they had to hold the chins up so that the windpipes were exposed. Then the blade was plunged in, almost to the hilt. That way there was maximum leverage for the cut across to the other side slicing, on the way, through the windpipe and the jugular vein, so that death was almost instantaneous.

They had to have the right tools, and they had to be of the highest calibre. It is a measure of an expert, in any field, that they know that choosing the best implement is part of being the best practitioner. Anyone who feels their skill is being disparaged because someone has said "you have very good equipment" doesn't understand this.

The knives came from the highest quality steel and the most reliable makers. There were no compromises. They were honed constantly to keep them as sharp as possible, so much so that in time the blades started to diminish in width around their centre of gravity. Then the cutting edge developed an S shape. That is the sign of a wicked knife.

The art of killing has a long pedigree. Slaughter in wars, in executions, judicial and otherwise, and in plain, old-fashioned murders, employed and employ the same methodologies as those that are affected in the charnel house. One tool that has spanned the full historic range of mammalian death dealing has been the poll-axe. Poll-axes are like the regular axes a woodcutter might use, but with this difference: the business end comprises of a tapered rod, which protrudes from a heavy cast-iron head piece. To ensure death with a poll-axe an experienced killer struck hard at the back of the head using the implement. The result of the strike was a hole of about the diameter of the smallest denomination coin in the skull of the victim, who collapsed with a roar. Into this hole the slayer inserted and withdrew a thin wooden dowel multiple times, which had the effect of scrambling the brain to make sure of death, but also of causing the limbs of the stricken to thrash about.

The poll-axe started as an instrument of war. Prior to the invention of gun powder, and the development of small-arms, one type or another was standard issue to armies all over the world. Sizes varied from small, single-handed implements for the use of mounted fighters, to a long-handled weapon with a head that contained a poll-axe on one side and a regular axe on the other, with a lance in the middle, for foot soldiers. This was known as a halberd. There are many instances where archaeological finds have uncovered human skeletons that bear the clear marks of execution by means of a poll-axe, particularly those close to battlefield sites.

In the slaughterhouse of the Considine brothers in their youths, slitting of throats was for sheep. Cattle were killed with the poleaxe.

- *Foreword to "The Makers' Name" by Seamus McKenna*

THE IRISH TIMES

24-28 TARA STREET, DUBLIN 2
Saturday, March 20th, 2021
irishtimes.com

Seasonal lamb

Sir, – As is becoming usual, The Irish Times has another fantastic picture on its front page (March 19th), courtesy of Laura Hutton.

The caption mentions that lambs are vulnerable during the first few months of every year. I have news: they are vulnerable for somewhat longer than that. There is a very high probability that the adorable creature in the photo will form the main constituent of a rack of lamb dish in the not-too-distant future.

– Yours, etc,
SEAMUS MCKENNA
Windy Arbour,
Dublin 14.

Chapter TWENTY THREE

Call for peace in Ukraine

On the 24th February 2023 a group of TDs and senators had a letter published in the Irish Times under their joint names. They acclaimed the principle of peace in that country, which is an irrelevancy, as who would argue for the opposite of peace?

The main thrust of the letter was that Ireland should call for peace negotiations, while pointing to its declared policy of neutrality, but the actual purpose was revealed in its penultimate paragraph. This read:

> "We reject those who are using this war to undermine Irish neutrality and move us towards Nato membership."

In other words, they were putting forward a totally futile and unrealistic proposition (calling on Vladimir Putin to cease and desist in his awful attack on Ukraine) in order to further their ideological standpoint (opposition to NATO and America's leading position in it). This argument took no account of the well-accepted facts that Ireland was not in a position to defend its neutrality. Our army is way under-strength, and at the last time of counting our navy was comprised of only two active ships. Our air corps (deliberately not called an airforce), has no fighter jets.

The signatories also ignored the fact that two countries which had previously been held up as exemplars of neutrality, Finland and Sweden, swiftly changed their policies on this matter after the Russian outrage against Ukraine, and applied for NATO membership.

The letter writers were roundly condemned, not just by me, but by all other letter writers that were published on that day in the Irish Times. The signatories to the politicians' letter were:

Senator FRANCES BLACK,
RICHARD BOYD
BARRETT TD,
Senator TOM CLONAN,
JOAN COLLINS TD,
CATHERINE
CONNOLLY TD,
Senator EILEEN
NÍ FHLOINN,
Senator ALICE-MARY
HIGGINS,
GINO KENNY TD,
THOMAS PRINGLE TD,
PAUL MURPHY TD,
Senator LYNN RUANE,
BRÍD SMITH TD,
Leinster House,
Dublin 2.

THE IRISH TIMES

24-28 TARA STREET, DUBLIN 2
Saturday, February 25th, 2023
irishtimes.com

Appeasing Russian aggression will not bring peace

Sir, – The letter from assorted TDs and Senators, replete with irrelevancies, truisms and non sequiturs, only has value in that it highlights the dangers inherent in having a letter written by a committee.

The letter's central thesis, which seems to be that Ukraine's best chance of promoting its right to self-determination and national sovereignty is by having its supporting nations attempt to appease the Russian despot Putin flies in the face of everything we should have learned from global history. – Yours, etc,
SEAMUS McKENNA,
Dublin 14.

Chapter TWENTY FOUR

Ursula von der Leyen and war in the Middle East

War in Gaza

The war that started after the incursion by Hamas fighters into southern Israel on October 7th 2023 has been devastating for the civilian population of the Gaza strip. It has also emboldened Israeli settlers in the occupied West Bank, who have accelerated their already nefarious work of harassing, dispossessing, and even killing Palestinian residents of the region.

These outrages have brought worldwide condemnation down on the state of Israel. It has also led to bitter criticism of its allies, particularly the United States of America, who provide the Jewish state with weapons and other war material.

The effects of the October 7th attack by Hamas were exacerbated by what seems to have been a terrible failure on the part of Israeli, US, and other western intelligence services, who are normally well informed about threats. Up to the day of the attack the lives of Israelis had become peaceful, almost to the point of tranquillity, after time had eased the trauma of previous outbreaks of violence.

The calm was such that it was felt acceptable to stage a music festival about 5.3 kilometres from the fence that separates the Gaza Strip from Israel. People attending this concert made up a sizeable proportion of those killed and injured in the Palestinian attack. In all, Israeli authorities have reported 1,300 people dead and 3,200 people injured, with about 240 hostages taken by the Palestinians back to Gaza. There have been allegations that many of the victims were raped and sexually assaulted.

Nearly eleven months after the Hamas attack only a small number of living hostages, and the dead bodies of many more, had been recovered. Very many Israeli citizens hold Benjamin Netanyahu to blame for this. In the Irish Times of August 24th 2024 their correspondent in Jerusalem, Mark Weiss, wrote:

"Some relatives [of the dead hostages] publicly blamed Mr. Netanyahu, saying their lives could have been saved if he had prioritised a ceasefire over saving his right-wing coalition."

The right-wing parties in that coalition are religious zealots, who support the activities of illegal settlers in The West Bank. Up to the time of the Hamas attack ordinary Israelis had prevented them from having political power. Now they are tolerated because a majority of the citizens of Israel fear for the very existence of their country.

Germany and Judaism in recent history

The recent history of the Jewish people and Germany is well-known. In the 1930s and into World War II they were picked out by Adolf Hitler's Nazi party to be the main victims of the drive to rid Europe (Nazis fully expected to rule all of Europe when the war was over) of those people that were regarded by them as being *Untermenschen* (subhuman), and ripe for elimination to make more room (*lebensraum*, or living space) for ethnic Germans and other Aryan peoples, so long as their mind set conformed to that of the Nazis.

Apart from the Jews, other races to be so dealt with included Roma (Gypsies) and Slavs (mainly ethnic Poles and those from the countries that now make up the Russian Federation). Communists and other groups that were ideologically opposed to Nazism were also singled out, as were individuals who had shown opposition to Hitler and his Nazi thugs. While they were at it, they decided to use the opportunity to eliminate even Germans who did not conform to their ideals of perfection, such as homosexuals and those with intellectual and physical disabilities.

The result was what has become known as The Holocaust. We mainly associate this term now with the death camps, where people were murdered on an industrial scale, but the build-up to the establishment of these was an absolutely horrific time for all who were targeted. As mentioned, the main focus was on the Jews, and when Nazi Germany invaded other countries their Jewish populations suffered enormously. Take, for example, the following two examples of what happened immediately after Operation Barbarossa, or the 1941 German invasion of the Soviet Union.

Evil in uniform

The photo below is a part of the record of an incredible, but well-documented, obscenity. It is also one of the most horrifying images of an actual event that I have ever seen.

There are about one hundred individuals in this picture. Most of the them are dead, and all but two will be dead in a short time. Those who will live are the only ones who are clothed. The paper whiteness of the bodies of the naked contrasts with the grey earth of the embankment that will be pushed over them to complete their mass grave.

In the moment that the camera shutter clicks all the victims are recumbent, but one young woman has raised the top part of her body using her left arm as support. What can be in her mind? Does she hold even the smallest, most pathetic, hope of escape? Near her a boy of about eight is almost in a sitting position. A little further back a dead woman has her arm in a protective gesture around a child, who is also dead. Standing over them all are two uniformed men with machine guns. The most prominent is, in the most matter-of-fact way, taking aim at the woman who has raised herself up on her elbow. When he has dealt with her he will, we expect, dispatch the youngster in the half sitting position. Or maybe his colleague behind him will take care of that detail.

This photo was taken during a mass murder of Jews at Babi Yar, outside Kyiv, in Ukraine, after the German army had invaded what was then the Soviet Union during the Second World War. Tens of thousands of people were murdered at this location over two days in 1941, in what would have been a well-planned and executed operation; Germany, then as now, had a reputation for efficiency.

The killers were under the command of the Waffen SS, the notorious military wing of the Nazi organisation. The shooters in the picture could have been SS, German special police or, more likely given what we can see of their uniforms, Ukrainian Fascist auxiliaries who had allied with the invading Germans.

For me, one of the most fascinating aspects of this and other, similar, photos is the question of who took them? It's easy to believe that some German army personnel would have travelled through occupied territory with a camera looped around their necks, ready to record events that occurred. But for them to see the subject matter of this photograph as just another interesting action on the fringes of the war they were in, is terrifying. They seem to have regarded what could be the most heinous crime in the history of humanity, the attempted obliteration, under the most hideous of conditions, of entire categories of men, women, and children, as just one more photo opportunity. That the pictures have even survived is a measure of their creators' callousness.

Finishing off Ukrainian Jews after a mass machine-gunning at Babi Yar, Ukraine, 1941.

Real horror

The most enthusiastic afficionados of horror movies must realise, unless they are children or those with the mental capacity of children, in which case they should not be exposed to them, that they are works of fiction. I contend that in that case they do not qualify as true horror at all. To conform to that terrible designation, they must be factual; they must show something that is happening, or that has happened in the past.

One of the most horrific photographs I know of shows torment and humiliation being inflicted on what looks to be a mature, respectable lady during an antisemitic outbreak in the city of Lviv in Ukraine in 1941, after the German invasion of the Soviet Union. Her outer clothing has been torn from her, and her undergarments are in disarray. These show, incidentally, the care with which she would have earlier in the day prepared herself for going out.

Her face is bloodied. That, and the state of undress, shows that serious violence had been inflicted on her before this photograph was taken. Her facial expression is one of sheer terror, and she is running as for her life. She can expect no assistance from the police or from anyone else. To compound the revulsion that any viewer must feel, she is being hunted by a baying mob of youths armed with cudgels.

What a truly awful scene this is.

Real horror in Lviv, 1941

Other victims

The Nazi regime in German had many victims. Apart from the 5.5 million Jews who were murdered in the death camps and in various killings like the one in Babi Yar described above, about 60 million people in total were estimated by some to have been killed and maimed before and during World War II. While many of these were combatants, from many nations, very many more were civilians; men, women and children.

But there was one more category of victim. This was the next generation of German and Japanese citizens. They bore a terrible burden of guilt, disgust, and national collective shame when they came to realise the truly terrible things that had been done by their immediate forebears. In Japan, militarism was outlawed by the constitution that was put in place after the war.

In Germany, the whole political landscape was transformed so that former Nazi operatives at all levels could be captured and put on trial. To offer come level of sympathy and sustenance to the survivors of Naziism, many in the new generation of Germans became supporters of the idea that Jews should have their own homeland. Ursula von der Leyen, who was deeply enmeshed in German politics, where she served as a cabinet minister as a member of Angela Merkel's CDU party before assuming her role as President of the European Commission, is one such. A staunch European, she is also, and firstly, a post-war German.

It was in this context that she, along with the President of the European Parliament, Roberta Metsola, of Malta, visited Israel on October 13th, some six days after the Oct. 7th attack. The purpose of the visit was, according to the two EU Institution Presidents, "to express solidarity with the Israeli people in the wake of the horrific Hamas terrorist attack."

At that stage the Netanyahu regime in Israel had not yet started on its the devastating military campaign in Gaza.

When the Israeli incursion into Gaza did get underway, and when the Israeli Defence Forces, or IDF, showed itself unable or unwilling to avoid enormous amounts of civilian death and maiming, including that of a great many children, commentators and opponents of Israel, and of Dr. von der Leyen, remembered the Oct 13th visit. She was strongly criticised for doing something that was of personal interest to her while she was deemed to be acting as the President of the EU Commission.

On December 14th 2023 Naomi O'Leary wrote a piece in the Irish Times entitled "Von der Leyen has torched her image in Ireland", wherein she quoted the words of a professor emeritus from Maynooth University who was critical of the Commission President. I responded with the following:

THE IRISH TIMES

24-28 TARA STREET, DUBLIN 2
Friday, December 15th, 2023
irishtimes.com

Von der Leyen's actions

Sir, – Naomi O'Leary ("Von der Leyen has torched her image in Ireland", December 14th) is wide of the mark if she believes the whole of Ireland's attitude to Ursula von der Leyen is reflected in the opinions of one professor in Maynooth, no matter how eminent. He does not speak for me.

Dr von der Leyen's actions have to be seen in context. As a German she, and a great many of her generation, are extremely sensitive to the fate of Israel because of the terrible things done to the Jewish population of Europe by their forebears during the first half of the last century.

Israel's modern tragedy is that its leadership is controlled by the outrageous Binyamin Netanyahu and his cohort of extreme right-wing bullies.

There is plenty of opposition to this leadership within Israel, as can be seen by anyone who reads its paper of record, Haaretz. This is the country's oldest surviving newspaper. (Its English language version is bundled with the New York Times international edition.)

The problem for all Netanyahu opposition now is that the Hamas attacks of October 7th were deeply traumatic within Israel, and led to the perception that the country is facing an outright existential crisis.

There is little doubt that if Dr von der Leyen had known what was about to happen to the civilian population of Gaza she would have been more circumspect regarding her decision to visit Israel after October 7th. But hindsight, of course, is a wonderful thing. This applies to university professors as much as to Irish Times columnists. – Yours, etc,
SEAMUS McKENNA,
Maynooth,
Co Kildare.

There was a follow-up to this particular discussion when the question arose about the definition of the word 'genocide'. I had the following in the Irish Times of December 19th, 2024.

THE IRISH TIMES

24-28 TARA STREET, DUBLIN 2
Thursday, December 19th, 2024
irishtimes.com

Ireland, Israel and international law

Sir, – Of course Ireland is not an anti-Semitic nation. Even members of the more responsible Israeli press acknowledge that ("Attention-grabbing gimmick? Israeli media reacts to Dublin embassy closure", News, December 18th). However, we do have anti-Semites in our midst.

Now the oppressed have become themselves oppressors, under the leadership of the cynical and callous Binyamin Netanyahu, who is kept in power by ultra-right religious zealots, a situation tolerated by the mass of right-thinking Israelis because of their perception that their country faces an existential threat, particularly after the outrages of October 7th, 2023, and the fact that the attackers on that date see it as acceptable to take and hold elderly people, women, and children as hostages, under presumed conditions that do not bear thinking about.

Criticism of the indiscriminate bombing of Gaza, and of the illegal and egregious actions of Israeli settlers in other parts of occupied Palestinian territory, should not be allowed to take from the historical monstrosity that was the Holocaust. For this reason seeking to change the currently accepted definition of the word "genocide", so that Israel can be accused of engaging in it, is wrong. We should have enough linguistic resources, here in Ireland of all places, to be able to think of another word. – Yours, etc,

SEAMUS McKENNA,
Maynooth,
Co Kildare.

Chapter TWENTY FIVE

Ireland in the European Union

In 1972 Ireland was finally allowed to enter what was then the European Economic Community, or EEC. Up to that time we had been denied access. This came about because the powers-that-be in France which, along with Germany, was the effective leader of the Community, did not want to allow Britain in, and Ireland's application was seen as inalterably bound up with that of our nearest neighbour. At that time our currency had a one-to-one fixed exchange rate with the Pound Sterling, and our two counties were tied together by the glue of a Common Travel Area.

Of course I was keen that Ireland should join, and events since then have convinced me all the more that this was a desirable outcome for our country.

Nevertheless, I suppose I have always also had a contrarian streak. This comes very much to the fore when everybody around me becomes what I believe to be overly enthusiastic for something. And this is what happened in 1972, when the French opposition to Britain joining was overcome, with the retirement of the French President, Charles de Gaul.

The journey to what eventually became the European Union was gradual, and uneven. It was initially the European Coal and Steel Community, and contained France, Italy, Belgium, The Netherlands, Luxemburg, and West Germany. This was created in 1950. In 1973 it became the European Economic Community (EEC), with the accession of Britain, Ireland, and Denmark.

The Maastricht Treaty

In 1993 the Maastricht Treaty created the European Union, whose form was further shaped by the Treaty of Nice. Later more countries joined. At this time of writing they number 27, after the secession of Britain on Brexit. Somewhat ironically, given that Ireland could not join the EEC without Britain, by the time of that country's departure Ireland had become a very strong member, and there was never any possibility that it was going to leave after that referendum in the UK.

Coming up to the treaty of Maastricht, and realising that there was quite a bit of opposition to this within Ireland at the time, I wrote the following letter to the Irish Times.

THE IRISH TIMES

24-28 TARA STREET, DUBLIN 2
13th June 1992

Sir, — In 1972, when the referendum for entry into the EEC was held, I took the view that it was being oversold by the government of the day, although I was broadly in favour of the Common Market. Accordingly, I voted "No" as a protest, to reduce the expected size of the "Yes" majority. In fact, I would have been horrified if we had not become members.

I believe that Maastricht is also being oversold. There is something distasteful about the concentration on £6 billion in aid to be supplied if we approve of the proposals, and it is certainly patronising to present the thing in such simplistic terms. However, I will not be indulging in the same kind of brinkmanship as in 1972.

I believe that this time around we need all the "Yes" votes that can be got. — Yours, etc.,
SEAMUS McKENNA,
Findrum,
Convoy,
Co Donegal.

Migration

The question of migration is one that has many layers. On the one hand there is the necessity, for humanitarian reasons, to assist people who are attempting to flee impossible situations, such as those brought about by war, famine, or natural disaster. On the other hand it is also true that western countries do not have the capacity to accommodate all who need help, particularly when their numbers are swollen by people who, because of the remarkable advances in communications technology, can see in real-time how attractive living in the West seems to be. These have become known as economic migrants.

But migration has other aspects too, and one of the most important of these is the question of integration. The term "multiculturalism" has been coined to apply to those people who elect to live in insulated pockets of population within the country to which they have migrated. In former times these would have been known as ghettoes. The word "ghetto" became a pejorative term as a result of their widespread use at the time in European cities for the incarceration of those who were ultimately bound for the death camps of Naziism.

Certain proponents of so-called multiculturalism maintain that it is not necessary for people living in such pockets to learn the language of their host country. This is not a good idea. It gives rise to all kinds of problems, not least of which is the difficulties that come about when the people concerned need to interact with the state in order to obtain benefits to which they are entitled, or to conform to the norms around having such things as a driving licence, or when medical treatment is indicated for them for conditions that are unknown in their country of origin, but which nevertheless can be very serious, or even life-threatening.

Integration does have to mean the elimination of culture. In fact, when migrants interact in a quotidian manner with those of the country to which they have come to live and to work, the people of the host nation also benefit, and significantly. There is then scope for a richness in the lives of all concerned. One of the best examples of this is in the incorporation of St. Patrick's Day into U.S. culture. While, prior to the time of the movement of a critical mass of Irish people to the US, it was unknown, it is now one of the highlights of the year there, and not just in New York, although the parade in that city is always a show-stopper.

In 2019 the European Parliament held a vote on a motion that was concerned with saving the lives of people adrift in the Mediterranean in unseaworthy boats. A provision of the resolution called for any ship with knowledge of the location of these vessels to let all concerned agencies have it. Four Fine Gael members of the European parliament voted against, on the grounds that they had a particular difficulty with the section that called for the sharing of information. They claimed 'they had been told' that to do so would assist people smugglers.

The motion was defeated by two votes. I made the following observation:

THE IRISH TIMES

24-28 TARA STREET, DUBLIN 2
Tuesday, October 29th, 2019
irishtimes.com

Search and rescue

Sir, – In France there is a law that makes it an offence not to assist people in danger (La non-assistance à personne en danger).

At sea, providing the location of a vessel that is at risk is fundamental to increasing the odds in favour of the success of the rescue effort.

It seems that the provision in the recent European Parliament resolution on search and rescue in the Mediterranean, to provide the location of vessels at risk, was included only because it was not contained in the legal codes of all member states. That this is so is a shame.

That Fine Gael MEPs of standing, such as Mairead McGuinness and Frances Fitzgerald, should vote down this proposal on the grounds that "they were told" that broadcasting the location of vessels in difficulty would in some way assist people smugglers, is outrageous. When one hears the phrase "we were told", one can be sure that the politicians concerned simply did not take the trouble to understand what they were voting for (Harry McGee, Home News, October 25th). – Yours, etc,
SEAMUS McKENNA,
Dublin 14.

French President Macron and European renewal

In advance of the European Parliament elections of 2019 President Macron of France had an article published in all of what was then the 28 members states of the EU; Britain had voted to leave, in the Brexit referendum, but had not yet done so.

In the article he argued strongly for the renewal of the idea of pooled sovereignty, so that the nationalist retrenchment instincts in certain of the member states would not derail the European project. The Brexit vote had taken place, and Britain was leaving the EU.

He reminded us that the EU "is a historic success: the reconciliation of a devastated continent in an unprecedented project of peace, prosperity and freedom."

He wrote "We should never forget that."

He went on to argue for the creation of a European defence capability, A European agency for the protection of democracy, which would provide each member state with European experts to protect their election processes against cyberattacks and manipulation, and the banning of the funding of European political parties by foreign powers. We should have stringent border controls.

Then he looked for a "social shield" for all workers, guaranteeing the same pay in the same workplace, and a minimum European wage appropriate to each country and discussed collectively each year.

He talked of the climate debt that we have built up over the years, and of the need to have zero carbon by 2050 and the halving of pesticides by 2025.

Europe needs to be able to look ahead to create jobs, to regulate the digital giants, and to finance innovation so that Europe can lead in new technological breakthroughs, such as artificial intelligence.

He wrote that "A world-oriented Europe needs to look towards Africa, with which we should enter into a covenant for the future, taking the same road and ambitiously and non-defensively supporting African development with such measures as investment, academic partnerships and education for girls."

Of course, I agreed with all of that. There was one thing niggling me, however. I had, over the years since the start of the EU, become concerned that it was managed in a manner that did not make it appear relevant to a large number of people. Perhaps that had to do with language; Irish people have developed a complacency with regard to learning other tongues, and this is probably brought about by the fact that we speak English, so we have been well able to communicate with our nearest large neighbour, and that most important trading nation on the other side of the Atlantic.

One way or the other, I thought the EU could do more to make itself appear relevant to the people that were its citizens.

THE IRISH TIMES

24-28 TARA STREET, DUBLIN 2
Wednesday, March 6th, 2019
irishtimes.com

Macron's call for European renewal

Sir, – French president Emmanuel Macron's words are all true ("Europe's renewal must be based on freedom, protection and progress", Opinion & Analysis, March 5th).

What he has left out, however, is significant. This is the insular bureaucracy of those charged with running the European Union over the years that has created a climate where the EU has seemed to be irrelevant in the lives of its citizens, which in turn has allowed the kind of potentially existential crisis that is Brexit to come about.

I hope the French president's unprecedented intervention is not too little, and not too late.

I hope that the situation that motivated it will galvanise him and others in positions of power in Europe to work towards more real involvement in its operations both for those who are enthusiastic Europeans, as well as for those who would otherwise hanker after narrow nationalistic outcomes. – Yours, etc,

SEAMUS McKENNA,
Windy Arbour,
Dublin 14.

Neutrality and The European Union

Then there was the letter that combined the subjects of neutrality on the one hand, and Ireland's place in the European Union on the other. I was able to make the following points:

THE IRISH TIMES

24-28 TARA STREET, DUBLIN 2
Tuesday, April 26th, 2022
irishtimes.com

Neutrality and public opinion

Sir, – I struggle to even imagine what Edward Horgan expects from the European Union when he says that it has "largely failed to promote peace within Europe, and especially within the wider world".

No EU member has ever attacked another, nor is there any indication whatever that this might happen. None has ever instigated any new colonial takeover since the inception of the union.

However, the EU has been instrumental in achieving peace in Northern Ireland, and especially in maintaining it in light of Brexit. That is as far as EU authority goes. It has no function or responsibility for what happens in any other part of the world.

The idea of "peaceful cooperation" with Putin's Russia, on anything other than that despot's terms, is nothing short of a joke, but a dangerous one: there are many other Putins out there waiting for their opportunity to dominate, and we need to be able to play our part in dealing with them in the only language they understand, which is military deterrence. – Yours, etc,
SEAMUS McKENNA,
Dublin 14.

Chapter TWENTY SIX

The physics of raindrops

The Irish Times letters page prides itself on its diversity. It is quick to print reposts to letters that have appeared, and it regularly carries challenges to its editorial stance. It also likes to embrace the esoteric.

On August 20th 1979, Noel Peart, of Monkstown, Dublin, made a simple query in the letters pages of the Irish Times. His question was well articulated; so much so that several other readers of the paper decided to attempt to answer it. I was one of them.

My studies at that time had been in Civil Engineering, at what was then the Regional College in Waterford, now the Sout East Technological University.

THE IRISH TIMES

13 D'OLIER STREET, DUBLIN 2
MONDAY, AUGUST 20, 1979

RAINDROPS

Sir,—I wonder if some of your readers could enlighten me on a subject which has been puzzling me for some time.

Sometimes, when I am walking in a mild shower of rain, all of a sudden the rain starts to come down really heavily. The drops beat off the tarmac and explode upwards. All pedestrians, even those with umbrellas, have to take shelter.

Now, this rain is not being shot down from the clouds; it is falling under the force of gravity. Assuming that the force of gravity remains constant, why do the raindrops start to fall faster?

It doesn't seem to have anything to do with the wind. I don't see why the drops should suddenly become larger, or heavier, and, indeed, I find it hard to believe that the drops would fall so much faster even if they did.

I am sure that somebody can help.—Yours etc.

NOEL PEART
1 Richmond Hill,
Monkstown,
Dublin.

First into the fray was F. E. Dixon of Terenure. He wrote as follows in an effort to resolve Mr. Peart's problem:

THE IRISH TIMES

13 D'OLIER STREET, DUBLIN 2
FRIDAY, AUGUST 24, 1979

RAINDROPS

Sir, — Noel Peart (August 20th), enquires why raindrops vary in falling speed, although the force of gravity does not change.

The falling speed is determined by several influences, notably the vertical movement of the air and the drag between the air and the raindrop. Raindrops are all small initially and can grow only if there is a strong updraught to keep them inside the parent cloud. When they eventually begin to fall, the speed increases until the drag balances the gravity acceleration. The raindrop then falls through the last few hundred metres (where the up - and - down air movements are small) at a uniform speed determined by its size, from 3 metres per second for a 1/2mm drop to 8m/s for one 5 1/2mm in diameter. Raindrops cannot grow beyond that size, as the drag forces break them up, but hailstones can grow larger and fall faster. — Yours, etc.,

F. E. DIXON
15 Terenure Road East,
Dublin 6.

On August 31st it was the turn of Henry Bacik from Cork. He wrote:

THE IRISH TIMES

FRIDAY, AUGUST 31, 1979
13 D'OLIER STREET, DUBLIN 2

RAINDROPS

Sir,—I would like to try to enlighten Mr Peart (as requested in his letter of August 20th) on the subject of the speed of raindrops.

A falling raindrop is subject to *two* forces: the force of gravity (constant), and a retarding force which is proportional to its speed. A raindrop of any given size will soon reach a speed at which these two forces on it are equal, and will then travel steadily at this speed until it hits a pedestrian, the ground, or other obstacle. This steady speed at which a raindrop travels is proportional to its diameter squared, i.e., a 2 mm raindrop will hit a pedestrian at four times the speed of a 1 mm drop.

Could this be the origin of the adage — "the bigger they are, the harder they fall"? — Yours, etc.,
HENRY BACIK.
Buxton Villa,
Sunday's Well Road,
Cork.

It looked as if that might have taken care of the business, but then, on September 5th 1979, along came Robert Kerr, from Ballinteer.

THE IRISH TIMES

13 D'OLIER STREET, DUBLIN 2
WEDNESDAY, SEPTEMBER 5, 1979

RAINDROPS

Sir, — With regard to Noel Peart's query (August 20th) re the speed of falling raindrops, might I be permitted to elaborate on F. E. Dixon's interesting, but somewhat confusing, reply?

Raindrops, just as any other bodies, would all fall with the same acceleration in a vacuum. However, falling through the atmosphere, they suffer from air resistance, and it is this resistance (due to the viscosity of the air) which effects the smaller drops proportionately more, and causes them to have lower velocities.

Both Mr Peart and Mr Dixon make one serious mistake: they assume the *force of gravity* to be constant. This is, of course, not true. It is the *acceleration due to gravity* which is constant. The force of gravity on a body is usually called its weight and thus depends directly on its mass. When the weight of the drop is exactly balanced out by the viscous force (given by Stokes' Law) the drop no longer accelerates, but moves with a constant speed, called its "terminal velocity." The terminal velocity of larger drops, then, is larger than that of the smaller droplets.

Continued...

...continued

For a full discussion of the reasons for drops attaining different sizes, the air flow pattern round different size drops, and the final disintegration of raindrops, might I refer the interested reader to B. J. Mason's article "Physics of a Raindrop." (Physics Bulletin, August, 1978). — Yours, etc.,
ROBERT KERR,
34 The View,
Woodpark,
Ballinteer,
Dublin 16.

And then Colin Murphy from Crumlin, Dublin, had his say:

THE IRISH TIMES

13 D'OLIER STREET, DUBLIN 2
THURSDAY. SEPTEMBER 6. 1979

RAINDROPS

Sir,—Regarding Mr Henry Bacik's letter of August 31st on the subject of raindrops, I would like to enlighten *him* as to the correct explanation.

He suggests that the difference in force between two raindrops striking the ground is related to a retarding force, by which I presume he means air resistance. However, his explanation would produce an effect totally opposite to that observed, as a larger retarding force would exist on larger raindrops and they would so strike the ground with less force.

The correct explanation is that the force with which a raindrop strikes the ground is not only a function of its acceleration due to gravity, which is constant, (gravitational *force* is not constant as he also suggests, but varies as the square of the inverse of the distance from the earth), but also its mass, and is given by the equation: Force = Mass x Acceleration.

Therefore, the raindrop of greater mass will strike with greater force. — Yours, etc..
COLIN MURPHY.
269 Cashel Road,
Crumlin.
Dublin 12.

It was at this stage that your humble servant got in on the act.

THE IRISH TIMES
13 D'OLIER STREET, DUBLIN 2
FRIDAY, SEPTEMBER 7, 1979

RAINDROPS

Sir,—I was surprised to see it asserted by Henry Bacik in *The Irish Times* of August 31st that the speed at which a raindrop travels towards the ground is proportional to its diameter squared. It seems, in my humble opinion, that the question of the speed of spherical falling bodies, such as raindrops, is a lot more complicated than Mr Bacik makes out.

The first factor, and mentioned by Mr Bacik, is gravitational attraction. Galileo, in a famous experiment, conducted from the Leaning Tower of Pisa, and later, Robert Boyle, in his laboratory, demonstrated that under the influence of gravity alone, the acceleration of bodies, and consequently their velocity after a given time, is independent of their mass and shape, i.e., if gravity were the only force working on two different-sized raindrops, and if they fell from the same height, their speeds would be exactly the same.

The second consideration then, and the one which will modify the speed of a large drop relative to a small one, is the effect of air resistance, again mentioned by your correspondent. The effects of air resistance are a consequence of the viscosity of the air, or the tendency of the air to retard the progress of the raindrops. This to the best of my knowledge, is proportional to the area of contact between the air and the drop. In other words, the larger the drop, and its surface area, the larger will be the retarding force. Also, viscosity depends upon the velocity of the body through the fluid (drop through the air) and the faster it would fall, the bigger would be the retarding tendency. On the other hand, however, because a larger drop would have a bigger mass, and consequently more momentum at a given speed than a small drop, it would tend to overcome the retarding force.

With all these forces interacting, and more esoteric ones such as the magnetic effects of electrically charged drops, I have severe doubts about whether a 2 mm raindrop hits the ground with anything like four times the speed of a 1 mm drop.

One other thing may be of interest. Force is equal to acceleration multiplied by mass. If a large drop and a small one hit an object at the same speed, they would naturally stop, and their deceleration or negative acceleration would be the same. This would mean that the larger drop, with its bigger mass, would strike with a force which would be greater, in proportion to the difference in mass, than the smaller one.—Yours, etc.,

SEAMUS McKENNA.
Seacliff,
Rectory Road,
Youghal,
Co. Cork.

But I was not to have the last word. That came from Kaare Breivik, of Malahide. It had been an interesting correspondence.

THE IRISH TIMES
13 D'OLIER STREET, DUBLIN 2.
TUESDAY, SEPTEMBER 18, 1979

RAINDROPS

Sir, — The forces acting on a falling raindrop are even more complex than indicated by Seamus McKenna (September 7th) and, as he suggests, the ultimate speed of a 2mm raindrop is nothing like four times the speed of a 1mm one. These speeds have in fact been measured and the figures I have at hand suggest that the speed of a raindrop of diameter 1mm is around 4.5 metres per second whereas one of 2mm diameter is 6.0 to 6.5 mps. Skin friction is not the only friction involved, as assumed by Mr McKenna. (This would require a laminar airflow around the droplets, which in turn requires a very low speed — such as may perhaps occur with very small cloud or fog droplets.) The speed of raindrops is so high that turbulent flow is created around them (and, indeed, within them), and the turbulence friction — far greater than the skin friction — will have to be added. The ultimate, constant speed of a raindrop, attained when this speed is such that all forces neutralise each other, increases with the size of the raindrop only up to a point: for drops larger than, say, 2 or 3 mm across, the speed soon levels out to reach a maximum of 8 or 9 mps for drops of diameter around 5.5 mm. The indications are that if the drops could grow larger still, their speed might even decrease. But such larger drops do not exist because at that size and that speed they are torn apart by the turbulence.

That the maximum observable speed is that found for raindrops which have grown to the maximum sustainable size is not so difficult to understand. But that the speed should actually level off is somewhat surprising. That this happens at the very same point where the drops have reached their maximum sustainable size is presumably just a coincidence.

The main factor causing this levelling - off of the speed may well be that falling raindrops become flattened by the air resistance. They are not spherical, nor even pear - shaped as so often depicted, but look more like fat, wobbly disks. Thus, a gallon of water, if it could remain in one piece, would probably float down relatively slowly like a flapping sheet or a weird - looking, jelly like creature from outer space, constantly changing its form. This contrasts with soft hailstones which, though usually spherical, often take the shape of cones with a spherical lower side, like the landing craft hitherto used by American astronauts. — Yours, etc.,

KAARE BREIVIK.
1 Yellow Walls Road,
Malahide,
Co. Dublin.

Chapter TWENTY SEVEN

AIB bank and remuneration

Directors' pay

Mathematics and physics go hand in hand. Years after the raindrops correspondence I read a news report on the money that had been paid to the directors of Allied Irish Bank, and the comment of its chairman to the effect that the increase in his remuneration from £5,000 in 1977, to £600,000 in 1995, was down to inflation. I decided to take him to task, and the Irish Times printed my letter.

There was an interesting follow-up to this. I received a letter to my home address from the same Mr. Culliton. I'm afraid it is no longer extant, but my memory tells me that the tone of it suggested that he believed I was a shareholder in the bank.

I loved that kind of thing.

THE IRISH TIMES

13 D'OLIER STREET, DUBLIN 2
THURSDAY, MAY 4, 1995

DIRECTORS' INTEREST

Sir, — Mr Jim Culliton, chairman of AIB group, is quoted (April 27th) as saying that the figures relating to directors' remuneration at his bank had given rise to "confusion".

I was certainly confused when I read his attempt to resolve the matter by saying that the amounts paid, "when adjusted for inflation", represented an increase of 13 per cent over the period between 1977 and 1994, and that this was "hardly of significance".

He also highlighted the fact that in the same period, the bank's profits had increased from £24 million to £341 million last year.

I was so confused I got out my spreadsheet and ran up a few calculations. According to my workings, anybody paid £5,000 in 1977, as Mr Culliton said the directors of AIB were, would have a compounded rate of increase over the seventeen years of 32.5 per cent, in order to reach the present level of directors' pay of £600,000. If the real rate of increase is 13 per cent, then the average rate of inflation over the period would have to be a whopping 28.75 per cent.

Maybe it was, but when we consider that the consumer price index has only risen by in the order of two per cent to three per cent in each of the last few years, then inflation would have had to be at extraordinary levels in the earlier years of the period to give Mr Culliton's result.

Perhaps Mr Culliton means that the rate of increase in directors' pay is 13 percentage points above the average rate of inflation since 1977. This would make average inflation over the period in question only (!) 19.5 per cent. But 13 percentage points over the rate of inflation, compounded for 17 years, is certainly not something that is "hardly of significance". As a banker, Mr Culliton should know a thing or two about the way rates and compounding work together.

Could it be that the best approach to getting rid of the "confusion" is to ignore inflation altogether and make a comparison? According to my figures, if bank profits had attained the same year-on-year increase since 1977 as directors' remuneration, then the bank would now be looking at a net margin of no less than £2.8 billion, compared to the measly £341 million it actually made. Could that be right? — Yours, etc.;

SEAMUS McKENNA,
Findrum,
Convoy,
Co Donegal.

Bonus payments

When the country was in the throes of the austerity that was designed to get us back on track after the financial crisis, and when the government was thrashing about looking for ways to save money, the Minister for Finance decided that he could cancel bonus payments to executives in Allied Irish Bank. That particular institution had been effectively taken over by the state, in return for the capital that was needed to keep it afloat.

I took exception to that.

Here I was then, arguing for the continuation of payments to people in AIB:

THE IRISH TIMES

24-28 TARA STREET, DUBLIN 2

FRIDAY, DECEMBER 17TH, 2010

Controversy over bonus payments

Madam, – Minister for Finance Brian Lenihan claims that a supervening event is the justification for cancelling the AIB bonuses, which were subject to contract. Surely this is exactly the argument the bank traders would use to have the payments made.

They were not responsible for the recession and, even if the were, it is hardly likely that such a circumstance was the subject of a clause in the contract.

How is it possible, given our property laws, to create legislation that will govern contracts in retrospect? Is it now open to commercial property tenants to claim the supervening event of the recession as a defence when their landlords take them to court to recover unpaid rents? Where will it stop? Is contract law to be thrown out the window?

A question for the bank: if these payments are contractual and definably related to production, why are they called bonuses at all? Does the logic of the Minister's action mean that piece workers in our few remaining manufacturing facilities are now susceptible to a similar action? Do certain salespeople run the risk of being confined to their meagre basic pay, which in some cases is actually nonexistent? – Yours, etc,

SEAMUS McKENNA,
Farrenboley Park,
Windy Arbour,
Dublin 14.

Chapter TWENTY EIGHT

Brussels, and airline practices

Between 1996 and 1997 I was fortunate enough to get a place on the full-time MBA course at Trinity College, Dublin. Was I the lucky fellow that I had a wife who has always been loyal and extremely supportive of my endeavours, and who also had a teacher's salary. Shane and Kate were in Primary School at that time. They all lived in Donegal, while I rented a room in a house in Palmerstown in Dublin.

I had a great time, but the year had to come to an end. Then I needed a job. I got one with Colgate-Palmolive company, in Brussels, Belgium.

At that time Ryanair was finding its feet. Its terminal for Brussels, which it grandiosely named Brussels South, was situated a full hour away by car or bus from the Belgian capital, outside the city of Charleroi. Aer Lingus flew into Brussels airport. The company had agreed to pay the air fare home by Aer Lingus for us ex-pats every two weeks but if we wanted to go home in the intervening weeks, while we were free to do so, we had to pay for it ourselves. The very large difference in the price of the flights between the budget, no-frills, Ryanair and the flag carrier meant myself and other Irish employees made the trip to Charleroi on those occasions; we also had the use of a car from a car pool for trips like that.

We found we had to turn up early for the Aer Lingus flights back to Brussels on Monday mornings because that airline was in the habit of overbooking. By doing this it could be sure the flight would be full, even if it had to disappoint some passengers who were already booked, and then compensate them. By overbooking they also made money from no-shows, of which there are apparently quite a few every year.

In those days there was an economy class and a business class on Aer Lingus flights. I took exception to this, largely on the grounds that, along with the practice of overbooking, it increased the likelihood that one would be told there were no places left even if one had reserved a seat.

I wrote the following letter to the Irish Times. The business-class service has now been discontinued on short-haul Aer Lingus flights.

THE IRISH TIMES

13 D'OLIER STREET, DUBLIN 2
WEDNESDAY, OCTOBER 28, 1998

BUSINESS CLASS FLIGHTS

Sir, — It has been reported that Delta Air in the US is about to abolish business class on its short haul flights. The given reason is that it will make more seats available, and is being driven by customer demand.

Aer Lingus should do the same, particularly on its Brussels service. Over-booking is now a fact of life on all busy flights, but it is intolerable that passengers who have a booking should be left behind, as happens almost every Monday on the 6:55 flight to Brussels, when the plane has had as many as 20 seats and more removed to pander to the vanity of those who want to travel first class.

Revenue considerations do not enter the equation. Whatever extra is paid for privilege would be at least, if not more, offset by the sale of the replaced seats.

The way business class is handled by, otherwise excellent, ground staff at embarkation is nothing short of a public relations disaster for Aer Lingus. It is galling to be told, over the public address system, that those passengers travelling in economy class will have to wait to board until those holding business class tickets have done so.

It is doubtful if steerage passengers on the Titanic felt as humiliated. Never mind that the result of putting those passengers to sit in the front on first, through the front door, leads to total chaos when the rest try to edge past people still placing their belongings in the overhead lockers.

I sometimes see Irish MEPs travelling to and from Brussels on these flights. On all occasions when I have noticed them, they travelled economy class. How democratic, I thought, and more evidence that so-called business class is extravagant and superfluous. I have since heard it alleged, by the BBC World Service, that MEPs are in the habit of claiming the expense allowance for a first class flight, then travelling economy and pocketing the difference. This is a cheap, tawdry fraud, if it happens. Yet another excellent argument for abolishing first class altogether.

There may be some merit in having a part of the plane reserved on very long flights for those who want more room and are prepared to pay for it. Even this would not be justified if it meant, as happens most Mondays on the Dublin to Brussels flight, that booked passengers would have to be left behind.

And one does not have to be a raving pinko communist fellow-traveller (pun intended) to find the idea of people being served champagne during a 90 minute commute to work on a Monday morning, just a little bit ridiculous. — Yours etc..

SEAMUS McKENNA
Avenue Louise,
Brussels,
Belgium.

Chapter TWENTY NINE

Energetic, resourceful, and hard-working students

By the time 2005 came around I was back in Ireland, after spending a number of years in both Belgium and The Netherlands working for Colgate-Palmolive company and Shell Oil. I was now involved in construction and property development, attempting to take advantage of what had come to be known as The Celtic Tiger, an appellation given to Ireland by an economist with investment bank Morgan Stanley in the title to a report on the Irish economy in 1994.

The term came into wide use as, after the report was published, the Irish economy only went from strength to strength. Foreign Direct Investment (FDI), or the coming to Ireland of many major multinational companies, as well as more than a few innovative ones, led to full employment and the gathering in of extraordinary amounts of money in Corporation and other taxes.

Then the banks discovered they could borrow at very low rates on the interbank market, and make loans at higher rates to developers and others (see above under Joke of the Week) at a very nice profit, which was further enhanced by arrangement fees. All of this led to even further economic activity.

But it was not to last. The days of reckoning came when the global economy collapsed, between 2008 and 2010, under the weight of very dodgy financial engineering activity that took place after the invention of mortgage-backed securities and a vast network of their derivatives, many of which relied on sub-prime mortgages for their existence.

But that was all in the future. In 2005 Shane and Kate were of the age when they would be thinking about university and in the throes of studying for and taking the exams that would get them there. Marilyn, a teacher, and I became very involved in informing ourselves about the possibilities open to our children in this regard.

A very attractive option for many young people was and still is the study of medicine. But this was very hard to get into. When it was suggested by a writer to the Times that it was somehow unfair to allow students to take the Leaving Certificate (the Irish equivalent of A Levels) over two years, my response was the following letter:

THE IRISH TIMES

10-16 D'Olier Street, Dublin 2
Thursday, August 25th, 2005

Repeat Leaving Cert students

Madam, – Your correspondent, John Hurley (August 23rd), argues that repeat Leaving Cert students compete for places in medicine under more favourable conditions than first-timers. Not true. There is a problem in medical training, but it is unfair to place responsibility for it on the shoulders of the highly motivated, energetic, resourceful and, above all, hard-working (attributes that some think should be present in those who qualify as doctors) young people who have realised that, as the system is currently structured, the only way to secure a place in medicine is to plan to do the Leaving Cert over two years instead of one. It is open to all to do this, so therefore there is no inequity.

The problem in medical training here is down to the extraordinary shortage of places, both in terms of demand and by comparison with other jurisdictions. There have been suggestions, in your paper, that this situation is exacerbated by the tendency of colleges to reserve places for non-EU candidates, from whom they receive much more in the way of fees than the amounts paid by the Government for university places under our free third-level education policy. Free education is a political principle and, as such, should be properly funded by the Government. This should certainly not be a problem in the current economic environment, where tax surpluses, in the order of many billions, are regularly recorded.

The Minister for Education has a responsibility in this matter. It was not encouraging to hear the incumbent, Mary Hanafin, make sympathetic noises but declare that she would do nothing without reference to the Minister for Health. The Minister for Health is not on another planet and we have the clear impression that Ms Hanafin is washing her hands of the problem. – Yours, etc,

SEAMUS MCKENNA,
Milford Cross,
Carlow.

Mary Hanafin, Minister for Education 2004 and 2008

The then Minister for Education was mentioned in the last letter. I'm afraid I had developed an attitude towards this particular politician, as I had gained the perception that she was very much in favour of allowing the religious indoctrination of children in schools. One acquaintance of mine had described her as The Minister for Catholic Education, and her actions and public pronouncements tended to confirm that, at least for me.

When it was announced that she was embarking on something that seemed to be a publicity stunt and not a serious effort to enhance the educational prospects of Irish children, I reacted accordingly, as follows:

THE IRISH TIMES

24-28 TARA STREET, DUBLIN 2
MONDAY, APRIL 14TH, 2008
www.ireland.com

Hanafin's free book scheme

Madam, – For a Minister of Education – who has already shown herself to be fond of gimmicks – to sending the gift of a book "with a note from the Minister" to every newborn in the State at a reported cost of €400,000 is a new low (*The Irish Times*, April 11th).

Of course reading is a fundamental skill. Of course children and their parents should be encouraged to take up and foster the habit. However, this report came a day after primary school managers highlighted the average €20,000 debt they carry. The expenditure reported would pay off the overdraft for 20 of our primary schools. Instead, parents in every county are reduced to fundraising on the streets to pay school electricity and water bills.

At the same time the pupil-teacher ratio is going in the wrong direction, in direct contradiction of undertakings given by Ms Hanafin and others.

The Minister and her Department should look to their priorities. Of course, this prompts the question: Is the number-one priority for this particular Department the creation of photo and other publicity opportunities for the Minister of Education? – Yours, etc,

SEAMUS McKENNA,
Farrenboley Park,
Dundrum,
Dublin 14.

Chapter THIRTY

Noise pollution

There are certain things in Ireland that seem to be taken for granted, things that would not be tolerated in other civilised countries.

People who have emigrated from Ireland to the US, and then returned, have testified that they were so complacent about the phenomenon of excess noise that they were amused when they discovered there were local ordinances banning the use of lawn mowers between certain hours, and outlawing motorised leaf blowers altogether. How We Laughed, they would report, about finding out about those things on their arrival stateside.

But We're Not Laughing Now, is the refrain when they have landed back in Ireland. This is because they have come to value, almost imperceptivity, the peace and tranquillity that such ordinances can give rise to. They were then exposed to business as usual at home; the aforementioned gardening machines, with the addition of chain saws, even on a Sunday; uncontrolled barking dogs; limited or no efforts being made by public works gangs to dampen the noise of jack hammers and compacters. I was in the walled garden in Kylemore Abbey once, on a Sunday, when a maintenance worker started up a petrol engine strimmer in order to clear grass from verges. The racket was intolerable. The operator had ear protectors, as is required by Health and Safety legislation, but no thought at all was given to the members of the public who were present. If one cannot find quiet in the walled garden of a working Benedictine abbey in Ireland, on a Sunday, where can it be found?

But the worst offender, for me, is the external bell intruder alarm. They're not bell noises anymore, of course, but have become the most distressing, and even injurious, sounds that modern electronic ingenuity can devise. They're made like that in the expectation that they will carry out an assault to deter a burglar, but all they actually do is cause extreme nuisance to ordinary people who happen to be in the vicinity. Collateral damage, the US military calls it, as when one of their ordnances has blown, not only the intended target, but also countless civilians in the neighbourhood, to bits.

The first letter I have on record on this topic dates from 2008. I had suffered terribly on that weekend. I counted no less than thirteen soundings of these alarms, not all from the same direction away from where I lived. On the Monday I called the local Garda station to see how many genuine break-ins there had been between the Friday and the Sunday. The answer was a great big, fat Zero.

Burglars do exist, of course, and it is a terrible thing to be the victim of one. However, the very same technology that gave us the horrendous noise when alarms go off can provide for monitored alarms, discreet cameras, and even communication that can inform the burglar, or the person with intent to burgle, that they have been seen, photographed and reported.

THE IRISH TIMES

Letters

Nuisance of house alarms

Wed Jun 04 2008 - 01:00

Madam, - A lovely weekend in Dublin has been disgracefully polluted, once again, by the unendurable noise of those intruder alarms that go off at all hours because of a puff of wind, or very often for no discernible reason at all.

It is well past time for the people who own and operate these devices be regarded as the bad neighbours that they are. If the Government were serious about both the comfort of the population at large and the genuine security of properties that need to have alarms fitted it would outlaw sound-only alarms and insist that all alarms are of the silent, monitored variety. - Yours, etc,

SEAMUS McKENNA,

Farrenboley Park,

Windy Arbour,

Dublin 14.

After the next letter appeared, which was some four years later, I was contacted directly by a gentleman who had been exposed to a nuisance alarm while he was in the process of doing some business in a shop in central Dublin. When he made a remark to the shop assistant about the almost intolerable noise, he was asked "What noise?"

> **THE IRISH TIMES**
>
> Letters
> # The 'war on silence' intensifies
>
> Fri Aug 31 2012
>
> Sir, – Over the past few years I have come to the conclusion that a majority of the Irish people are partially deaf. This is the only explanation for the general lack of sympathy for those who suffer significantly from the many noise sources mentioned in Colm Keena's article.
>
> Faulty, badly fitted or ill-maintained intruder alarms and barking dogs are two things that are of particular concern.
>
> Those citizens that possess normal or sensitive hearing are an oppressed minority. It is therefore up to the Government to protect their wellbeing.
>
> At the very least, the statutory 20 minutes that false alarms are allowed to sound should be reduced to five minutes. – Yours, etc,
>
> SEAMUS McKENNA,
> Farrenboley Park,
> Windy Arbour, Dublin 14.

Then, in 2016, Marilyn and I returned from a holiday in Portugal. The place where we stayed had lots of high-end properties, and they did have signs warning that security was in place. But we never, ever, heard an intruder alarm going off.

THE IRISH TIMES

Letters

The 'war on silence' intensifies

Fri Aug 31 2012

Sir, – Over the past few years I have come to the conclusion that a majority of the Irish people are partially deaf. This is the only explanation for the general lack of sympathy for those who suffer significantly from the many noise sources mentioned in Colm Keena's article.

Faulty, badly fitted or ill-maintained intruder alarms and barking dogs are two things that are of particular concern.

Those citizens that possess normal or sensitive hearing are an oppressed minority. It is therefore up to the Government to protect their wellbeing.

At the very least, the statutory 20 minutes that false alarms are allowed to sound should be reduced to five minutes. – Yours, etc,

SEAMUS McKENNA,
Farrenboley Park,
Windy Arbour, Dublin 14.

Chapter THIRTY ONE

China

In 2008 a controversy started over Tibet its treatment by China. It was brought on by Green Party, who apparently invited the Chinese ambassador to a meeting, which was then critical of his country. A Mr. Kevin Lynch from Drumcondra, who seemed to know what he was writing about, had something to say about that.

He made a point that I had often pondered on. This was the tendency of many Irish people to be critical of countries they had never visited. In the olden days their opinions would have been shaped by Roman Catholic propaganda; the idea that all countries that tried the Communist method of governance were atheistic, and therefore evil. This alone would have turned everybody's minds against China and the USSR, regardless of what efforts these countries had made to better the lives of their citizens. Cuba would have fallen into this category, despite the fact that it is well recognised to have one of the world's best health services.

Mr. Lynch's letter is worth reproducing in full in order to get an understanding of what was happening:

THE IRISH TIMES

13 D'OLIER STREET, DUBLIN 2
WEDNESDAY APRIL 16TH 2008

China, Tibet and the Green Party

Madam, – Having read John Gormley's comments at the weekend and having watched RTÉ's *Questions & Answers* on Monday night, I am astounded by the hypocrisy of both Western media and politicians towards China. No doubt this stems from fear and misunderstanding of the globe's new economic and political superpower.

Apart from the damage that Mr Gormley's remarks will do to an already failing Irish economy, his behaviour toward the Chinese ambassador was a disgrace and nothing more than a costly publicity stunt by the Green Party.

Rather than using the correct diplomatic channels to discuss the Tibetan issue with Chinese diplomats, Mr Gormley invited the Chinese Ambassador to a public meeting and then insulted him. This was the worst kind of grandstanding, as his remarks will do nothing for Tibet and nothing for Ireland.

While Mr Gormley is being feted as a hero in his own party for standing up to China, the reality is that he has damaged Ireland's good standing with China to serve his own ends. For example, the rules for Irish nationals applying for Chinese visas have now been altered by the Chinese Embassy, as of Monday.

Some of the comments about China, mostly from people who have never even set foot there, highlight the ignorance of the country and its people. How many people are aware that a Tibetan Autonomous Prefecture (TAP) already exists near Western Sichuan in China? And that it is where most Tibetans live peacefully? And that it has the largest Lamist monastery in the world with more than 500 Lamist monks? And that the Dalai Lama himself favours this type of autonomy?

China has come very far in very short time in terms of modernisation and the problems that do

Continued...

> **...continued**
>
> exist cannot be fixed overnight. But rather than trying to understand the Chinese position, the ill-informed anti-China agenda seeks to alienate, insult and humiliate a proud people and a country that is trying to resolve these issues.
>
> Perhaps, before criticising China or indeed any other country, Irish people should look at the disgraceful treatment of Irish boxer John Joe Nevin last Friday. Having qualified for the Beijing Olympics, he was unable to book a "welcome home" function in any hotel in Cavan or Mullingar because he is a settled traveller.
>
> Did John Gormley have any comment on this denial of human rights at his party's convention? – Yours, etc,
> KEVIN LYNCH,
> Drumcondra,
> Dublin 9.

His letter was the cue for me to get in on the act. I had for some time been thinking about the inexorable rise in the world's population. Reading the letter I perceive that I regarded overpopulation as even more important than global warming. Thinking about it now, I feel that each of these things has the potential to exacerbate the other, with incalculable consequences for the migration crises that are now beginning to be an issue for the developed world. Global warming will displace more people, and overpopulation will ensure that there are even more people to be displaced.

THE IRISH TIMES
Friday, April 18, 2008

China, Tibet and the Green Party

Madam, – Kevin Lynch is right (April 16th). China has come a long way in a very short time. It also leads the world in population control. The Chinese minister of the State Commission of Population and Family Planning has claimed that the one-child-per couple policy has resulted in 400 million fewer births than would otherwise have been the case. That's equivalent to about 80 per cent of the current total of men, women and children in all member-states of the EU.

Not too far in the future, the rest of the world will salute China for this achievement. In a world where, at the current rate of expansion, the human population grows by a billion people every 11 years, and where it is set to double in the next 60 years, this problem makes global warming and climate change seem almost trivial by comparison. Of course, the doubling will not take place. Either population growth will be curtailed in other countries as it has been in China, or massive famines, on a scale never seen before, will occur.

I hope the Green Party is aware of this issue. – Yours, etc,
SEAMUS McKENNA,
Farrenboley Park,
Dublin 14.

Visit of Xi Jinping to Ireland, 2012

When he was vice-President of China, Mr. Xi Jinping made a visit to Ireland along with large trade delegation. He came from the US, but Ireland was the only member state of the EU that was favoured with his presence on this occasion. It was well known that Mr. Xi was on track to be the Premier of China, which would make him the head of one of the most powerful countries in the world.

He was met by the Taoiseach, Enda Kenny, and entertained royally. His entourage consisted of 150 individuals, and was made up of both government officials and people from trade agencies. A number of agreements were signed at Dublin Castle, and this was overseen by Mr Xi and the Taoiseach. Before that he had been taken on a tour of the attractions that Ireland has to offer. The delegation visited a Shannon Development business park, took part in a traditional Irish banquet at Bunratty Castle; they visited a dairy farm, and then went to the Cliffs of Moher. After that it was off to Dublin where they went to Croke Park. The Chinese leader was photographed trying his hand at both hurling and Gaelic football.

To round things off there was a special performance of Riverdance. This show has already proved to be very popular with Chinese audiences at home.

The question of Tibet was raised during the vice-President's visit.

During one contribution it was stated that no less than 36 Tibetan monks have deliberately burned themselves to death in protests against the Chinese. That seemed to me to be a totally disproportionate response to whatever grievance the Tibetan monks have. I thought that they, along with certain other nationalities that have religion at their core, and who are oppressed, must have a culture of martyrdom. This can only be possible if you really and truly believe that there is a life after death, and that entering into that afterlife in the most painful manner possible is the best way to ensure that you will be in the right place after you have left this life.

THE IRISH TIMES

Letters

China's human rights record

Wed Feb 22 2012

Sir, – The visit of the Chinese vice-president makes it incumbent on all of us to become better informed about this massive nation which is assuming a global role it did not have in the past, and its related issues. And it would appear that the question of Tibet is relevant, as reflected in the letter by Anthony O'Brien of the Tibet Support Group Ireland (February 21st).

But there was one jarring note in that missive for me. Mr O'Brien says that a total of 36 Tibetans have self-immolated in the recent past. Am I the only one to feel that suicide is not really an appropriate form of protest, and that the decision to self-immolate is a choice that is made by the person concerned and not something that is imposed on him or her by the Chinese? – Yours, etc,

SEAMUS MCKENNA,
Farrenboley Park,
Windy Arbour,
Dublin 14.

China was also mentioned in a letter I wrote about population control, in 2014. I believe it speaks for itself:

THE IRISH TIMES

24-28 TARA STREET, DUBLIN 2
Tuesday, September 2nd, 2014
irishtimes.com

Population policies

Sir, – The naiveté demonstrated by Rev Patrick G Burke with regard to population growth is breathtaking (September 1st). His example of us not being knee deep in flies when we should have been if all the offspring of one breeding pair had survived and bred ignores the reasons why this did not happen – great fly populations were wiped out by a variety of means, which in human terms have corresponded to famines and genocidal wars interspersed with periods of low life expectancy and miserable health experiences.

The continent of Africa, for which he quotes figures, is no stranger to famine, genocidal wars, low life expectancy and miserable health experiences.

He talks of over 200 years of "lived experience". Does he not realise that 200 years represents a mere millisecond in terms of the time humans have been reproducing? Does he not know that the increase in people on the planet in the past 50 years has exceeded the population growth up to that time in all of the ages since the first humans appeared?

He mentions Malthus. This man's theories have never been disproved. And there is very strong evidence to suggest that, unless policies such as those adopted by China are implemented, it will only be a matter of time before they will receive as much recognition as those of Darwin and Einstein. No matter how much we increase food production by scientific means, the production capacity of the Earth still remains a finite quantity.

Some acquaintance with mathematical principles, which explain exactly what finite means (and also Malthus's invocation of exponential growth) would greatly inform debates such as this one. – Yours, etc,
SEAMUS McKENNA,
Farrenboley Park,
Windy Arbour,
Dublin 14.

Chapter THIRTY TWO

The Waterford Blaa

THE IRISH TIMES

24-28 TARA STREET, DUBLIN 2
Monday, November 25th, 2013
irishtimes.com

Blaa breakthrough

Sir, – It is gratifying that the blaa, forever associated with my home town and eagerly sought after on my occasional visits there, has been given European recognition as to its source. But I must take issue with Eddie Hearne (November 21st) when he says it was introduced by French immigrants.

There are a number of problems with this theory. For a start, there were much bigger Huguenot communities in other Irish cities, most notably Dublin, and the unique and tasty bap never appeared anywhere other than in Waterford. Also, when I was a cutter in Waterford Crystal (better known locally as "The Glass" in those days) I was told by another cutter, one McEvoy, that the blaa had been started in the Gold Crust bakery, now also sadly defunct, by bakers who wanted what would, in the present day, be called a mini-loaf to have with their tea in the middle of the night, when all the bread was baked.

McEvoy knew this because his father was one of the bakers.
– Yours, etc,
SEAMUS McKENNA,
Farrenboley Park,
Windy Arbour,
Dublin 14.

Thousands of small, soft, white, floury confections, supplemented by the preferences of the eater, are consumed in Waterford and its environs every day. These are known as blaas, and are unique to Waterford City and its immediate surroundings. They are delicious and will be on the must-have list of anyone who grew up in or around Waterford when they return for visits. Everyone has their own favourite type and filling. A crusty blaa, well buttered, and containing sliced tomato covered in Cheese and Onion crisps, is the favourite of your humble servant.

Describing the blaa can very well be left to the Official Journal of the European Union, which has declared that the delicacy is entitled to protected status with regard to its geographical origin, which is known as the EU Protected Designation of Origin, or PDO. From the Official Journal:

> *"Description of product to which the name ... applies*
>
> 'Waterford Blaa'/'Blaa' is a soft doughy white bread roll clearly identified by the white floury top on the product.
>
> The bread has the following characteristics:
>
> ### Shape
>
> 'Waterford Blaa'/'Blaa' can be round or square. They are made both crusty and soft and are pinned out round and trayed up round but they batch together as they expand during baking, when they are pulled apart they are square shaped but their domed top gives them a round appearance.
>
> ### Size
>
> 'Waterford Blaa'/'Blaa' is 3-4,5 cm high with a diameter of 8-12 cm and weighs 40-65 g."

All of this gives the name Blaa the same geographical protection as that afforded to, for example, Champagne.

The region in which the geographical designation is valid for the blaa is also defined in the EU Journal:

"Concise definition of the geographical area

The geographical area is restricted to the geographical area known as all of County Waterford and that part of South County Kilkenny, which directly adjoins County Waterford made up of the Ullid and Dunkitt electoral divisions which is part of the southern Piltown electoral area. The river Blackwater runs through the area and includes the town-lands of Dangan, Narabawn, Moolum, Newtown, Skeard, Greenvilleand and Ullid."

It is when the journal deals with the history of the blaa that it runs into trouble. It claims, no doubt having been briefed by present-day Waterford blaa producers, that it dates from the arrival of the Huguenots, Protestant refugees from France in the seventeenth century. The EU journal is careful to point out that written records in Waterford have been lost, and that the story is dependent on local oral history.

Large numbers of this Protestant sect left France after the revocation, by King Louis the Fourteenth, in 1685, of the Edict of Nantes, which had given them protection from religious persecution. They moved to those parts of Europe that were Protestant. There were many Huguenot communities established in the then British Isles, which at the time included the whole of the island of Ireland, where the established religion was the Anglican (Protestant) Church of Ireland.

The Huguenot theory for the origin of the blaa would imply that the floury delicacy was not of Waterford origin at all. It would be akin to claiming that Champaign originated somewhere other than in the region whose name it bears. And it does not stand up to historical scrutiny. The Huguenot Society of Great Britain and Ireland has it that:

"The refugees went mainly to neighbouring Protestant states such as Holland, Switzerland, Germany and Great Britain, as well as Ireland. Smaller numbers moved on to settlements in the European colonies of America and South Africa".

The blaa is not known in any of those places. Neither is it associated with other towns and cities in Ireland that accommodated Huguenots. Many of these have "French churches" that date from this period, but no blaas. According to the Society, some 5000 individuals came to Ireland. They established sizeable communities in about 20 locations throughout the land.

The probable real story of the origin of the Waterford blaa is more prosaic than the Huguenot theory. It has, however, the priceless attribute of establishing that it was invented in Waterford, by Waterford people.

One or two Waterford natives have long held that they know a lot about the origin of the blaa. One claimed that his father, a baker in Gold Crust bakery, a venerable old Waterford institution that is unfortunately no more, had often told him that he and his colleagues had been in the habit of using the dough left over, after the following day's bread had been baked, to prepare a batch of small baps for consumption with their tea after the night's work. They were smothered in flour and buttered before they were eaten, and this concoction became the blaa that we all know and love. It was not long before other bakeries followed suit, and one or two of them even began to specialise in blaas.

There is no need to gild the lily about the origin of the blaa. Here we have something that is indeed unique to the region, and which has been deemed so by the European Union. Why take the risk of having its origin moved elsewhere? Moved perhaps, like Champagne, to a location in France?

Chapter THIRTY THREE

Wine bottles

There are a number of things to consider when one takes up the subject of wine bottles. Their shape, of course, their capacity, and the manner in which they are sealed so that the precious contents are not in danger of release unless that is what is intended. But for me the most impressive aspect of the regular 75 centilitre bottle is its longevity, and ubiquity. It seems that this container has been around for millennia.

This volume of wine is perfect for consumption by two people if they have also the enjoyment of a meal and a conversation over it, while it is ideal for one person if there is no companion other than, for example, a good book when the meal is under way.

Of course, there are exceptions to the rules. There always are. Take the shape. While there is almost consensus by wine producers that their nectar should be supplied in a regular cylindrical glass container with a cross sectional diameter that is roughly that of the breath of an adult closed fist, a certain Portuguese vineyard, with a speciality in rosé wine, long ago broke away from that accord, and began to supply theirs in bottles that have a strange, elliptical bulk, the greatest consequence of which has been their inability to be placed in conventional wine racks of the sort that most people use outside of the catering trades, and indeed inside them as well.

There has long been debate within the ranks of connoisseurs about the merits and demerits of cork versus screwcap for the sealing of the bottle. Traditionalists, of which there are many in places like France, regard the screwcap in much the same way as a medieval bishop might have regarded a heretic. On the other hand, wine imbibers of a more pragmatic bent welcome the metal interloper because there is, in its use, no danger of the chemical reaction that can sometimes result in the contents being 'corked' and thereby rendered undrinkable.

As in many aspects of life, it seems, you pays your money and you takes your choice.

THE IRISH TIMES

24-28 TARA STREET, DUBLIN 2
Tuesday, March 22nd, 2022
irishtimes.com

Wine bottles – put a cork in it?

Sir, – Around the Faubourg-Montmartre area of Paris, which I visited recently, they do not have any time for screw-cap wine bottles. Are they all purists, or is this a protective measure to support the cork-stopper industry?

Cork-stoppers come from the bark of the cork oak tree, the harvesting of which can only be carried out by specialists. This is to ensure that the tree, which can live for up to 300 years, will not have its trunk damaged. Then the bark will grow back, ready to be harvested again in future years.

In all of the establishments selling wine, and there are many, there was not a screw-cap to be seen.

My own attitude to the phasing out of the cork at home is largely one of indifference. I am very ready and willing to make use of a corkscrew, but I have also had some excellent libations from bottles that did not require one. I have noticed one thing: there is a tendency, at dinner, to replace the screw cap after the wine glasses have been charged, which is something one would never do if a cork had been extracted. This can make for some mirth around the table on those occasions when the time for a refill arrives and the expected slosh of the life-enhancing liquid fails to materialise from the mouth of the bottle suspended over the glass.

Even here, there is a compensation – all too often I have made the mistake, as the evening has advanced, of pouring white wine into the partially full water glass of the intended recipient.

Forgetting to remove the cap allows for a retake, in which this mistake is then less likely to be made. – Is mise,
SEAMUS McKENNA,
Dublin 14.

Chapter THIRTY FOUR

Censorship of books and other publications

The depredations of the Irish Censorship of Publications Board, which was set up as one of the provisions of the various Censorship of Publications Acts, are well known. Started originally in 1929, a new act was introduced in 1947 so that in the 1950s, under the law, thousands of books, periodicals and even newspapers could not be imported or sold. Gardai visited bookshops and removed publications that were on the banned list. Many of these were international classics of literature, such as J.D Salinger's The Catcher in The Rye, East of Eden, by John Steinbeck, and The Heart of the Matter, by Graham Greene, among many, many more.

A particular irony lay in the fact that, while some Irish authors were enjoying spectacular success abroad, their books were banned in their native country. Among these Irish writers were Edna O'Brien, Brendan Behan, and John McGahern.

Book censorship in Ireland was insidious. Apart from the official censorship board, many in the book trade were active in making sure that only those titles they thought were fit for public consumption were allowed to be sold. In 1938, when Patrick Kavanagh published his book, The Green Fool, he found that a number of prominent bookshops in Dublin refused to stock it on the grounds that it criticised the Catholic Church.

Kavanagh was a colourful character. He went to these shops and created a disturbance; he had come to the conclusion that there was a conspiracy against him. The Guards were called. A sergeant made a report to help in deciding what to do about the matter. Then he consulted with a priest! The priest was of the opinion that if Kavenagh were to be prosecuted it would only create publicity, which would tend to increase demand for the book. So, the matter was dropped.

In 2017, after censorship had ceased in Ireland, to all intents and purposes, a report was published that said an English schoolmaster had banned certain books from his school library. I wrote the following, rather tongue in cheek, response to this.

THE IRISH TIMES

24-28 TARA STREET, DUBLIN 2
Friday, March 31st, 2017
irishtimes.com

Libraries and banning books

Sir, – Of course the censorship of books that do not openly advocate hate or crime is wrong. However, reading Lorraine Levis's piece ("Headmaster bans 'brutal, banal' Irish books from UK school's library", Culture, Online, March 29th), I cannot help thinking about the experience of readers or budding readers in the middle years of the last century in Ireland.

At that time almost any book that had any merit, including those by Irish giants of literature such as John McGahern, Edna O'Brien, and many others, were banned by the official censor. Our response was to crave these publications much more than might otherwise be the case, and to do whatever was required in order to obtain them. Then they had to be read in secret and hidden in between times.

But the effort was well worth it, and added greatly to the enjoyment; forbidden fruit does indeed taste better.

In light of this it is worth considering that the action of the headmaster who is the subject of the report actually constitutes a cunning plan, the aim of which is to motivate children to read more, not less. – Yours, etc,

SEAMUS McKENNA,
Windy Arbour,
Dublin 14.

Chapter THIRTY FIVE

And on the subject of books…

It is not at all remarkable that a writer would also have a life-long interest in reading. This one is no exception. But in 2013 I was successful in having a somewhat tongue-in-cheek comment on the subject published. It went down rather well with my regular readers.

THE IRISH TIMES

24-28 TARA STREET, DUBLIN 2
Tuesday, December 28th, 2021
irishtimes.com

A turn-up for the books

Sir, – Books are great. Not only can they be savoured and enjoyed if well written, but they can impart knowledge and information even if poorly done. Sizeable hardback books are by far the best items for propping up The Irish Times at the breakfast table in the morning; they have ballast, and the height can be fine-tuned to perfection by the simple expedient of adding or removing one or more of them.

And you know when you're on a video conference call and you are particular about the relationship of the camera on your laptop to the upper part of your body – I like to have the little eye at the exact same height as my face so that I am perceived to have a steady, level gaze by the other participants – then the only practical answer is a small pile of books. This year Santa brought me quite a few of them. – Yours, etc,
  SEAMUS McKENNA,
  Dublin 14.

About the author

As a Civil Engineer he was involved in harbour development, the building of a natural gas platform, and many large construction projects. He obtained an MBA from Trinity College, Dublin in 1996, after which his career went international. He returned to Ireland to play a part in the Celtic Tiger years of financial and investment excess, when he became involved in construction and property development. This all came crashing down when the global financial crisis of 2008 – 2010 hit. His novel, THE MAKER'S NAME, while a work of fiction, takes inspiration from his career experiences.

From 1978 he has been having his letters published in the Irish Times newspaper. Those letters are the basis for his book "THE RECONSTITUTION OF IRELAND: Separation of church and state, and other topics, through the letters pages of The Irish Times", which argues for the removal of religious discrimination from the Irish public system, particularly as it applies to schools.

He is the author of the Omicron Forex Trading Manual, a best-selling treatment of algorithmic Foreign Exchange trading. His letters and articles, on a wide range of topics, have been published in the Irish

Times and in other publications over many years. In 2023 he was awarded a Master's Degree in Creative Writing by Dublin City University (DCU).

On 21st July 2024 he broadcast his short-form piece "Chickens, Hurling and a Famous Bootmaker" on RTE Radio 1's Sunday Miscellany programme (New writing for radio).

Leave a review

Reviews are important for any book. Many thanks indeed to all who have supplied one for my previous work, *The Maker's Name*. I would be extremely grateful if readers of *The Reconstitution of Ireland* could find the time to put fingers to keyboards now and send them in. There are three sites for reviews. The top one at this time is Goodreads, but Amazon and Barnes & Noble are also very important. The same review uploaded to each would be great.

Sincerely

Seamus McKenna

Index

A

abortion, 2, 3, 12, 43, 113, 118, 121, 123, 124, 161
Abraham Lincoln, 15
Africa, 14, 211, 251
agnostic, 18
artificial intelligence, 211
atheist, 18
Austerity, 150

B

bank directors' pay, 2
Baptism, 14
Bastille, 29
BBC, 24
Belfast, 29
Bertie Ahern, 28, 31
bishops, 15, 20, 55, 70
blaa, 249, 250, 251
Black, 14
blasphemy, 3, 50, 51
bloody", 5
Bobby Sands, 9, 10
Bogside, The, 8
books, 3, 5, 255, 256
Brendan Behan, 255
Brexit, 2, 206, 211
business class flights, 2

C

cardinals, 15
Catcher in The Rye, 255
Catholic Church, 3, 6, 11, 12, 15, 40, 41, 48, 54, 58, 61, 64, 67, 69, 82, 84, 88, 96, 101, 104, 113, 114, 123, 162, 255
celibacy, 3, 96
Celtic Tiger, 148, 166, 230, 259
Censorship, 255
Censorship of Publications Board, 255
Charles, Prince of Wales, 12
child abuse, 2, 3, 93, 101, 104
China, 26, 241, 244, 247
church and state, iii, 2, 3, 4, 28, 36, 47, 56, 63, 259
Civil Service, 6
climate debt, 211
Cloyne report, 18, 93, 104
coercive behaviour, 6
coercive control, 6
conditioning, 14, 18
Constitution, 6, 12, 19, 47, 48, 50, 53, 61, 64, 86, 113, 163, 176
Constitution of Ireland, 6, 48, 50
contraception, 6, 19, 20
contraceptives, 19, 20
Corporal punishment, 15
counselling, 17, 175

D

Daniel Dennett, 18
Darwin's Dangerous Idea, 18
Dawkins, 18
De La Salle, 16, 67
Declan Kiberd, 166
democracy, 2, 20, 28, 64, 211
democratic republic, 3, 104
Derry, 8, 9, 10, 11
Diana, Princess of Wales, 12
discrimination, 3, 260
divorce, 2, 6, 7, 8, 11, 12, 24
Donald Trump, 3, 176, 180, 182, 184, 186
Donegal, 8, 9, 24, 26, 128, 129, 227
Dublin airport, 173
Dublin Area Rapid Transport, 173
Dunblane, Scotland, 24
Dustin Hoffman, 24

E

East of Eden, 255
economics, 2
Edna O'Brien, 255
education, 2, 3, 4, 6, 14, 36, 45, 53, 54, 55, 56, 58, 59, 61, 63, 67, 70, 72, 75, 76, 81, 82, 86, 94, 96, 101, 166, 211
Eighth Amendment, 2, 118
embryos, 3, 113, 114, 117, 118
emigration, 15
Europe, 48, 196, 211, 250
European Economic Community (EEC), 2, 206
European Union, 2, 150, 205, 206, 213
Eurozone banking system, 150
evolution, 17

F

Family Law in the Republic of Ireland, 7
financial crisis of 2008, 150, 259
Fine Gael, 7, 161, 209
Fintan O'Toole, 28, 30, 59, 70, 75, 101, 180, 182
France, 51, 64, 205, 211, 250, 251, 253
freedom of speech, 2
freedom to travel, 3
French Revolution, 29
From Dusk till Dawn, 24

G

Gerry Adams, 130, 133
Gerry Adams and the N-word, 133
God Delusion, 18
God is Not Great, 18, 31
Graham Greene, 255

H

Hanafin
    Mary, 233
Hans Kung, 20
hare, 2, 145, 146
hare coursing, 2, 145
Hare coursing, 145
Heart of the Matter, 255
Heineken cup, 136
hereditary monarchy, 29
High Court, 19
Hitchens, 18, 31
HIV/AIDS, 20
homosexuality, 12, 41
Huguenot, 250, 251
Humanae Vitae, 20, 22
hunger strike, 9

I

Industrial Development Authority, 8, 25, 158
Integration, 208
international affairs, 2
Ireland, i, iii, iv, 2, 3, 5, 8, 9, 11, 12, 14, 15, 18, 19, 24, 29, 40, 43, 44, 47, 48, 50, 51, 53, 54, 55, 56, 64, 70, 75, 79, 82, 89, 93, 96, 101, 104, 107, 113, 123, 125, 128, 129, 133, 139, 140, 143, 147, 148, 150, 153, 155, 157, 158, 161, 162, 166, 173, 180,184, 192, 203, 205, 206, 213, 230, 244, 245, 255, 256, 259
Irish Film Censor's Office, 24
Irish military neutrality, 2
Irish Times, iii, 1, 3, 4, 11, 24, 28, 31, 37, 40, 47, 53, 56, 58, 67, 70, 79, 82, 88, 94, 99, 102, 114, 130, 139, 142, 145, 151, 166, 176, 178, 186, 192, 193, 196, 203, 206, 214, 223, 228, 259, 260
island of saints and scholars, 158

J

J.D Salinger, 255
John McGahern, 38, 255
John Steinbeck, 255
Joke of the week, 147
Judeo-Christian ethic, 24

L

Leinster Rugby, 136
Letter to a Christian Nation, 18
libraries, 5
Lifford, 8
Luduvic Kennedy, 18

M

Maastricht Treaty, 206
Macron, 211
Macron, President, 211
Mary McAleese, 11, 40
mass shootings, 2, 24
McGee case, 19
Mediterranean, 209
Migration, 208
minorities, 2, 20, 118
Mother Teresa, 12
multiculturalism, 208

N

Naked Ape, by Desmond Morris, 17
Neutrality, 213
noise pollution, 2
Northern Ireland, 8, 12, 29

O

oath, 3, 44
Omicron Forex Trading Manual, ii, 260

P

paedophile, 17
parish priest, 5
Patrick Kavanagh, 255
Patrick Kavanagh published his book, The Green Fool, 255
politics, 1, 2, 28, 168, 169, 178, 180, 202
Port Arthur, Australia, 24
Presbyterians, 29, 55
property prices, 2
Protestant, 29, 55, 250, 251

Protestant Unionist, 29
Provisional IRA, 9, 129

Q

Quenten Tarantino, 133

R

raindrops, 2, 223
raindrops, physics of, 214
referendum, 11, 12, 48, 51, 113, 153, 206, 211
Repeal the Eighth, 3
representative government, 29
responsible adults, 14
rhythm method, 20
Roman Catholic hierarchy, 6
Roman Catholicism, 29, 48
Russia, 151
Russian aggression, 3

S

Sam Harris, 18
Samuel L. Jackson, 133
science, 2, 37, 159
Science, 158
Seanad, 2
secular state, 3, 44
secularism, 3, 28, 31, 63, 64
sex, 3, 17, 72
Sexual abuse, 16
sexual activities of consenting adults, 12
Shatter, Alan, 8, 11
Sheamus Smith, 24
St. Patrick's Day, 180, 208
Strabane, Co. Tyrone, 8
Sunday Miscellany, ii, 260
Supreme Court, 19, 49, 114, 176

T

Taoiseach, 28, 53, 104, 161, 180, 184, 244
Taoiseach, Bertie, 28

Temple Street children's hospital, 136
The Bogside, 9
Thomas Jefferson, 28, 47, 48
Tom Garvin, 166
Troubles, 9, 128
Turkeys voting for Christmas.\, 6

U

United Irishmen, 28, 29

V

violence, 2, 6, 24, 41, 163, 164, 195, 200

W

Waterford, 17, 67, 110, 176, 214, 248, 249, 250, 251
Waterford Blaa, 248
wine, 3, 252, 253
wine bottle cork, 3
Wine bottles, 252

X

X case, 3, 113, 118

Y

Youghal, 8
YouTube, 24

More recent letters to the editor

THE IRISH TIMES

24-28 TARA STREET, DUBLIN 2
Saturday, November 8th, 2025
irishtimes.com

Lesson for the Tánaiste

Sir, – In his victory speech after his win in the New York mayoral election, Zohran Mamdani said: "New York will remain a city of immigrants, a city built by immigrants, powered by immigrants and, as of tonight, led by an immigrant."

He might have added that a very, very high proportion of those immigrants came from Ireland. They came to flee famine, they came to flee oppression because of their revolutionary activities, and they came, yes, to improve their economic situation. In other words, many were economic migrants.

When in New York they contributed greatly to the political, commercial and administrative life of the city.

Then, earlier this week we had the Department of Finance Future Forty report which, according to your own editorial on November 4th, made the point that "immigrant labour will continue to be needed in the workforce".

In light of the above it is disappointing indeed to hear the leader of Fine Gael, the party of Garret FitzGerald and Declan Costello, claiming, on the basis of spurious figures and for reasons known only to himself, that: "There are too many people who come to this country and who are told they do not have a right to be here and it is taking too long for them to be removed."

The tone was oppressive and the claim was incorrect. The fact of the matter is that we have rules about immigration in this country and, crucially, these rules are being followed, even if tardily.

Tánaiste Simon Harris would need to cop himself on. – Yours, etc,
SEAMUS McKENNA
Maynooth
Co Kildare

THE IRISH TIMES

24-28 TARA STREET, DUBLIN 2
Friday, May 9th, 2025
irishtimes.com

Religion in the classroom

Sir, – Paddy Monahan of Education Equality has written a very powerful piece (Opinion, Thursday, May 8th) on the need to have faith formation moved outside of our classrooms. It has all been said before, of course, and it is shocking, in this day and age, that it is necessary to keep on reiterating the need for what is a basic requirement in an otherwise diverse, open-minded, and anti-discriminatory society.

The article reminds us that, at least up to now, the needs and opinions of that most important element of our educational establishment, the teachers, have been ignored. Perhaps, at last, they will find themselves in a position to affect the outcome, just as the camogie players have found it possible to make their voices heard over the rigid demands of those who would appeal to "tradition" to impede proper progress. – Yours, etc,
SEAMUS McKENNA,
Maynooth,
Co Kildare.

From the same author:

The Considine brothers, Rudi and Gus, are at war.

Their father, Malachi, has died in a 'freak accident'. But is there such a thing as a freak accident? When Rudi attempts to grab Gus's inheritance there's a real prospect of human blood appearing on the Hawthorne Meats slaughterhouse floor. Enter Cosgrave, a solicitor with expensive tastes, and Toomarood, the banker with an eye to making money outside of his day job. Mix in the 'free' energy device, after experts have stated that the promoters are suffering from long-term, severe self-delusion. Does this all make up a catastrophe waiting to happen?

To be published in March 2026:

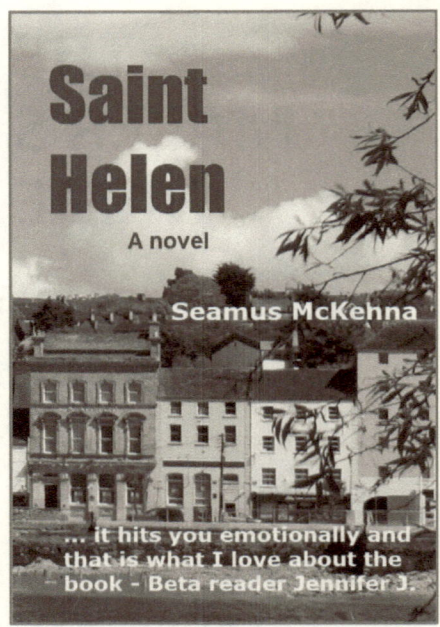

In the spring of 1975, Engineer Anton Quigley arrives to assist in the construction of an offshore gas rig platform in what was then highly conservative and judgmental southern Ireland.

He falls for Helen Peavoy, a courageous teacher. But her real love is the enigmatic Ned Rocket, a member of Sinn Féin, the political wing of the IRA. When she becomes pregnant by him her world spirals. Then a terrible outrage is committed by the IRA; everyone's loyalty is tested. Anton must confront his feelings, and struggle internally to maintain his integrity.

Will genuine true love overcome the turmoil?

See all at: www.seamusmckenna.ie

www.ingramcontent.com/pod-product-compliance
Lightning Source LLC
Chambersburg PA
CBHW030227100526
44585CB00012BA/274